The Management
Speaker's Handbook

Practical books that inspire

2-4-6-8 How Do You Communicate?
How to make your point in just a minute

Making an After Dinner Speech
How to make a speech that has them rolling in the aisles

Powerful Business Speeches
How to motivate and persuade – whatever the business situation

Appraising Job Performance
*Key assessment techniques that will
positively influence motivation*

Speaking in Public
Speak out with confidence and make a winning speech

howtobooks

Please send for a free copy of the latest catalogue:

How To Books
3 Newtec Place, Magdalen Road,
Oxford OX4 1RE, United Kingdom
email: info@howtobooks.co.uk
http://www.howtobooks.co.uk

The Management Speaker's Handbook

Templates, ideas and sample material
that will transform every speaking occasion

Patrick Forsyth

'The human brain starts working the moment you are born and never stops until you stand up to speak in public.'

Sir George Jessel

Published by How To Books Ltd,
3 Newtec Place, Magdalen Road,
Oxford OX4 1RE. United Kingdom.
Tel: (01865) 793806. Fax: (01865) 248780.
email: info@howtobooks.co.uk
http://www.howtobooks.co.uk

British Library Cataloguing in Publication Data
A catalogue record for this book is available from the British Library

Cover design by Baseline Arts Ltd, Oxford
Produced for How To Books by Deer Park Productions
Typeset by PDQ Typesetting, Newcastle-under-Lyme, Staffs.
Printed and bound by Cromwell Press, Trowbridge, Wiltshire.

NOTE: The material contained in this book is set out in good faith for general guidance and no liability can be accepted for loss or expense incurred as a result of relying in particular circumstances on statements made in the book. The laws and regulations are complex and liable to change, and readers should check the current position with the relevant authorities before making personal arrangements.

Contents

Preface

'It usually takes me more than three weeks
to prepare a good impromptu speech.'

Mark Twain

If someone had said, early in my career, that I would
earn my future living largely by speaking in public I
would have dismissed the thought out of hand. I could
not do it, did know how to do it and did not *want* to do
it. The very thought terrified me. However, events led me
in a direction that meant I *had* to do it – and this, in
turn, meant I had to learn how to do it.

I still remember my first public speech with horror. But
this is a skill that most managers must do and do well;
and it is one that *can* be learnt. Given the apprehension
many people feel at the thought of public speaking (if it
makes you nervous, then you are normal!), looking for a
little guidance is only sensible. Consider the task. It is all
too easy for the ill-prepared presenter to go to pieces:

They stumble, they hesitate, they sweat. They begin
every sentence with the word 'basically'. They say *'Um,
er...at this moment in time we are making considerable
progress with the necessary preliminary work prior to
the establishment of the initial phase of the project'*
when they mean *'We will begin soon'*.

Just when they should be blinding their audience with

their expertise, they upset or confuse them. At worst they go on too long, their explanation is inadequate, they pick holes in their audience or, worse still, their noses. Their slides cannot be read from the back of the room without a telescope and the only long word of which they are manifestly ignorant is apparently 'rehearsal'. They are struggling, and they know it.

For some people making a potent, powerful, persuasive presentation is second nature. They know their stuff and how to put it over. Their first rule is to assume the audience is as thick as they look and will, provided they hit the right level of impenetrable jargon, instantly conclude they are in the presence of an expert.

Because they want people to understand the gist of their argument they talk down to their audience. They talk v-e-r-y-s-l-o-w-l-y; use simple words and generally treat the audience as if they had the brains of dormice. They spell out complicated bits by talking IN CAPITAL LETTERS. They need only the briefest of introductions and they are away, moving quickly past the first – upside down – slide and rattling the coins in their pocket at 90 decibels. Blissfully ignorant of the fact that they are alienating their audience they seem to think that they can survive stepping into the lion's den just by saying 'Nice pussycat'.

I exaggerate somewhat... I think. More seriously, no audience will warm to a speaker who is ill prepared and who flounders through a talk that is poorly constructed and inexpertly delivered. The task must be approached from the basis of some understanding, some thought as to what might best be said and how it might best be put over, and with respect for the task, the audience and an eye on what must be achieved. It can be a daunting task.

This book is designed to help whether you face having to speak for the first time or if you have both some experience and proven competence. Part One covers concise and practical advice on the techniques of presentation. Part Two provides specific guidance in the form of a blueprint for a variety of individual speaking situations. These sections can provide a quick check before you tackle a particular occasion; they also contain information, advice, and useful quotations that will extend your confidence for any speaking task.

I wish I had had something like this many years ago when I first started to speak and present in public. As will become clear as you read on, success on your feet is not a matter of good luck, so I will not wish you that – but I wish you well with whatever presentations you find yourself undertaking.

Patrick Forsyth
Touchstone Training & Consultancy
28 Saltcote Maltings
Maldon
Essex CM9 4QP
United Kingdom

About the Author

Given the topic of this book it is perhaps appropriate to mention the author's credentials in offering advice in this area. Patrick Forsyth runs *Touchstone Training & Consultancy*, an independent firm specialising in the improvement of business performance, and focusing primarily on marketing, sales, communications and management skills.

As a consultant and trainer of more than 25 years' experience, Patrick has fronted a great variety of events. As a trainer he has led many management training events. Many for individual companies and others in the form of public seminars for organisations such as The Institute of Management (and similar bodies overseas, for example The Singapore Institute of Management). He has also spoken at many conferences, some public events, some for specialist bodies such as Central Law Training and others for individual companies. Training has involved him in addressing audiences ranging from a dozen people from one company to several hundred from many different organisations. One major event involved an audience of more than two thousand plus video links to more people in other cities. He also has spoken at events where simultaneous translation has been used to relay what he said (or the gist of it!) to non-English speaking audiences.

His training work has always included many workshops designed to develop participants' skills in making effective presentations. In addition, among a number of successful books he has written, two other books are on this topic *Hook your audience* – the latter looking at the use of anecdotes and examples to enhance or enliven business presentations.

Like most presenters he has found that things have not always gone well. He has on occasion been the only person to make it to an event (because of heavy snow); opened his file at the start of a presentation to find material for a different event in front of him; lectured by candlelight in a power-cut and paused for various venue catastrophes ranging from fire alarms (real and imaginary) to falling ceilings. Despite such occurrences he continues to make presentations and tries hard to remember the advice of David Martin: *The golden rule for all presenters is to imagine that you are in the audience.*

PART ONE
INTRODUCTION

CHAPTER 1

Key Approaches to the Task of Presentation

'Take care of the sense, and the sounds will take care of themselves.'

Lewis Carroll

Good morning, Ladies and Gentlemen ... Wait a moment, there is a good deal to think about before you reach that stage and actually rise to your feet and speak. Making a presentation effective necessitates a number of things, not least doing some preparation. As a starting point it is worth stepping back and focusing on some of the core elements of communication.

First consider the way in which a message is taken in. Comprehension is not a straightforward process, many aspects combine to make it more difficult than it might otherwise seem. Surely, if you know your subject there should be no great problem putting over something that people will understand? Actually, this may not be the case. Communication presents difficulties that are inherent, and stem in the main from five areas:

1. **How people hear** or rather, how they sometimes do not hear. People find it difficult to concentrate for long periods, their minds flit about (as yours is doing, perhaps, reading this). This means that messages must be delivered in a way that repeatedly keeps

demanding attention. In addition, people make assumptions about the importance of what they hear. They will reject some points, or 'tune out' for a moment if it does not clearly appear to be an important or interesting part of the message.

2. **How people understand:** understanding is always diluted:

   ◆ if matters are not spelt out clearly or are confused with jargon. Jargon is professional shorthand, useful when everyone knows it to the same degree, confusing if not – and important because it becomes a habit, one that can take a conscious effort to avoid when necessary;

   ◆ because people misunderstand more easily what they hear, but do not see; hence the importance of visual aids;

   ◆ because people draw conclusions ahead of the completion of the message, and do so because the sense appears clear to them;

   ◆ and because people make assumptions based on past experience: *'Ah, that's like so and so'* they say to themselves, when in fact it is not, or proves not to be as the full message is spelt out.

3. **How people change their views:** business presentations often involve asking people to change their viewpoint,

often a long-held one. This creates suspicion, the same feeling that we sometimes recognise when we deal with someone with 'something to sell'. Additionally, people dislike being proved wrong, and the acceptance of a new view may imply a past mistake in believing something else. Therefore the communication has to be pitched just right to overcome this factor.

4. **How people decide to act:** change, of course, is a good thing; who wants to be thought of as a 'stick in the mud'? And so it is; but just try going into the office tomorrow and saying '*Right, there are going to be some changes round here, now*' and see what response you get. People, for the most part, make changes reluctantly. They do not like changing habits, they are fearful of making wrong decisions, and of the results of so doing. These are all good reasons for ensuring careful communication.

5. **How feedback occurs:** all the former factors would be easier if we always knew accurately what was going on, how much of the message was being taken in. But people often hide their reactions, and are protective about what they are thinking, at least in the short term. This is true even to the point where feelings are actively disguised, a nod rather than a 'Yes' in fact indicating puzzlement rather than understanding or agreement. Feedback may well be 'on hold' for much of a presentation, and a speaker can only judge

reactions from the general feel and look of the group they are addressing.

What is generally happening here is that any message is going to be filtered as it is received. It is checked for validity, for relevance, to see if it relates to previous experience or clashes with any prejudices, and is then probably only accepted in diluted form. If the communication is good it will get through unscathed, or largely so; if not there are many hazards waiting to make it less effective.

As ex-President Nixon is attributed with saying: '*I know that you understand what you think I said, but I am not sure you realise that what you heard is not what I meant.*'

Overcoming the difficulties

All of this means that the business communicator must be careful to communicate in ways that will overcome all, or most, of these difficulties. Particularly, it is wise to:

◆ Bear in mind the kind of audience you have, especially if in terms of beliefs or experience they are likely to see matters in a way that is different from you.

◆ Make sure that the meaning of what you want to put across is clear; even the wrong or poor choice of one word can change what you want to say. I once heard someone in a presentation describe his organisation as offering *'a fragmented range of services'*. Whatever he meant (divisionalised for better communication with customers, perhaps), it was the wrong word, and the negative impact on those to whom he was speaking was all too clear. Yet it was just one word; greater confusion will place the message further off target. The danger of jargon, which is also relevant here, has already been mentioned.

◆ Visual aids, which allow you to utilise two senses and add the variety of changing between one and the other, are clearly useful, and it is rare for an event of any length not to include any.

Any good communication is, in part, a matter of attention to detail; more so in a presentation. Just using one word instead of another can make a slight difference. Actually, just using one word instead of another can make a *significant* difference. And there are plenty of other factors that contribute, many of which are explored further on in this book. But there are also certain overall factors that are of major influence, and which can be used to condition your communications. These are simply a reflection of human nature, they are inherent (and link to what, more formally, psychologists call the laws of learning – they help people take something in and make it more likely they will retain it).

These include:

The 'What about me?' factor

Any message is more likely to be listened to and accepted if the way in which it will affect people is spelt out to them. Whatever the effect, in whatever way (and it may be ways) people want to know – *what's in it for me?* and *how will it hurt me?* people are interested in both the potential positive and negative effects. Tell people that you have a new computerised reporting system and they may well think the worst. Certainly their reaction is unlikely to be simply – *good for you.* It is more likely to be – *sounds like that will be complicated* or – *bet that will have teething troubles or take up more time.* Tell them they are going to find it faster and easier to submit returns using the new system. Add that it is already drawing good reactions in another department, and you spell out the message and what the effects on them will be alongside each other, rather than leaving people wary or asking questions.

Whatever you say, bear in mind that people view it in this kind of way. Build in the answers and you avert their potential suspicion and make them more likely to want to take the message on board.

The 'That's logical' factor

The sequence and structure of communication is very important. If people know what it is, understand why it was chosen and believe it will work *for them*, then they will pay more attention. Conversely, if it is unclear or illogical then they worry about it, and this takes their mind off listening. Something like this book makes an example: it might be possible to have a chapter investigating the fundamental principles of communication towards the end of the book, and a reason for it; but I doubt it. Certainly readers would query it and look for a good reason.

Information is remembered and used in an order – you only have to try saying your own telephone number as quickly backwards as you do forwards to demonstrate thi. So if your selection of a sensible order for communication makes sense to people, again they will warm to the message. Using an appropriate sequence helps gain understanding and makes it easier for people to retain and use information.

Telling people what is coming is called signposting. Say – *let me give you some details about what the reorganisation is, when the changes will come into effect and how we will gain from it* – and, provided that makes sense to your staff, they will *want* to hear what comes next. So tell them about the reorganisation and then move on. It is almost impossible to overuse signposting. It can lead into a message, giving an overview, and also separately lead into sub-sections of that message. Sometimes it can be strengthened by explaining why the order has been chosen – *let's go through it chronologically, perhaps I could spell out . . .* – within the phrase.

Whatever you have to say, think about what you say first, second, third and so on and make the order you choose an appropriate sequence for the staff to whom you are communicating.

The 'I can relate to that' factor

Imagine a description: it was a wonderful sunset. What does it make you think of? Well, – a sunset, you may say. But how do you do this? You recall sunsets you have seen in the past and what you imagine draws on that memory, conjuring up what is probably a composite based on many memories. Because it is reasonable to assume that you have seen a sunset, and enjoyed the experience in the past, I can be fairly certain that a brief description will put what I want in your mind.

It is, in fact, almost impossible not to allow related things to come into your mind as you take in a message (try it now: and *do not* think about a long, cool refreshing drink. See?). This fact about the way in which the human mind works must be allowed for and used to promote clear understanding.

On the other hand, if I was to ask you to call to mind, say, the house in which I live and yet describe it to you not at all, then this is impossible; at least unless you have been there or discussed the matter with me previously. All you can do is guess, wildly perhaps – *all authors live in a garret – all authors are rich and live in mansions –* (and here this is wrong on both counts!).

So, with this factor also inherent in communication, it is useful to try to judge carefully the extent of people's prior experience; or indeed to ask about it if they have not worked for you for long and you are unsure of their past experience. You may also refer to it with phrases linking what you are saying to the experience of the other person. For example, saying things like – *this is like* .... – *you will remember* .... – *do you know* ...? *this is similar, but* - all designed to help the listener grasp what you are saying more easily and more accurately.

Beware of getting at cross purposes because you think someone has a frame of reference for something which they do not; link to their experience and use it to reinforce your message.

The 'Again and again' factor

Repetition is a fundamental help to grasping a point. Repetition is a fundamental help to .... Sorry. It *is* true, but it does not imply just saying the same thing, in the same words, repeatedly. Repetition takes a number of forms:

◆ Things repeated in different ways (or at different stages of the same conversation).

◆ Points made in more than one manner: for example, being spoken and written down (or shown on a slide).

◆ Using summaries or checklists to recap key points.

◆ Reminders over a period of time (maybe varying the method, for example, phone, fax or meeting).

This can be overdone (as in the introduction to this point here), but it is also a genuinely valuable aid to getting the message across, especially when used with the other factors now mentioned. People really are more likely to retain what they take in more than once. Enough repetition.

Making a presentation

Let us focus again more specifically on making a presentation. What makes a good presentation? There is one overriding factor: empathy, the ability to put yourself in the shoes of the participants. Most of what makes people say '*That's a good presenter*' is down to this in one way or another. There is no academic measure – a good presenter is simply one whom the audience likes, and in a business context finds useful; and in training for instance it is one from whom they learn – preferably something of value – in an interesting way. Whatever you are trying to do must aim to create audience satisfaction; even breaking bad news may be judged appropriately and sensitively done.

So you must think about how you see the audience (whoever they may be – and each is different), and how they see you. As the latter is more straightforward, let us start with that.

How the group sees you

Any business presenter must direct the group, must be in charge, and must therefore look the part. There are some people who hold that the presenter should always wear a suit, or the equivalent in terms of formality for a woman. Certainly appearance in this sense is important, though it should link to the culture in which the presentation takes place. Similarly, you should normally stand up as opposed to sitting (there may be some sessions that can be run while sitting, but not many and these are less our concern here). Not only does appearance differ, but most people will actually perform in a different and more stimulating manner when standing. If standing is the chosen option, stand up straight, do not move about too much, and present an appearance of purposefulness.

The speaker is the expert, is, or should be, in charge, and so appearance is a relevant factor.

How you see the group

How you view the group is not, of course, simply a visual point; what is necessary is an understanding of the group, and the individuals in it, and an appreciation of their point of view and their way of seeing things. Presentations may well demand decisions of people. Do I agree? Can I see the relevance of this? Shall I agree with this point? So it is necessary to understand the thinking process which takes place in the minds of those in the group in such circumstances.

This thinking follows a common sense sequence of seven stages (originally documented by psychologists in America and paraphrased here). Each stage is important to how a message is received, and a successful presenter will bear them all in mind. We now review these stages to illustrate how they affect what must be done.

1. I am important

We all regard ourselves as important, and what is more we want others to recognise this importance. Unless the presenter is seen to respect members of the group, communication will not be completely successful and if action is required it may not take place. This process must occur directly in terms of normal courtesies, and in terms of the way to which the jobs, responsibilities and performance of the people are referred. One important implication here is that you should never be condescending (you *do know* what condescending means don't you? – sorry, I could not resist, but hope the point is made; talking down to people is always resented).

2. Consider my needs

Needs in terms of what people feel as individuals, and relative to the jobs they do (clearly, these are sometimes in conflict, as with a message designed to prompt action that will improve job performance but which will perhaps be difficult for the individual); both aspects are important. Attention will always be greater and more immediately given if it is made absolutely clear how what is being presented relates to people's needs.

3. Will your ideas help me?

If what is being said is beginning to be seen as relevant, then an analysis takes place which asks if it is actually something to accept and implement, either literally or in some modified form. Does it, in fact, meet needs that exist? People weigh up what is being said, looking at the facts and seeing if any of them indicate snags.

4. What are the facts?

With much of what will be put over in a presentation, participants are not making a snap judgement, though sometimes this will tend to happen, but are intent on weighing up the case to see whether they are convinced. They therefore want to know the facts, and they want them logically presented in a form that assists the weighing-up process. They ask themselves whether they have enough information, the right information, and whether they are clear about it – do they understand to a degree that will allow the message, whatever it is, to be accepted and/or implemented?

5. What are the snags?

There are always two sides to any argument. The phrase 'weighing up' used earlier was deliberately chosen; this is exactly what is happening. Members of the group will ask themselves both what are the reasons to accept this, and what are the points against? Often there are snags, but they do not necessarily rule out acceptance – on balance, they may conclude, the case is good. Any snags likely to be perceived in this way need either to be anticipated, and commented upon to redress the balance put over in the presentation or, if reservations come up as questions, they need to be handled effectively with the same aim in mind. It is unrealistic with many presentations to think that no objections will be raised.

5. What shall I do?

Here the process of implementation is also in play. In other words, having weighed up the case – assessed the balance – people not only need to be able to say '*I accept that point*', nor even '*I accept that point and will do it*'. They may need to be able to say '*I accept that, I will do it and I can see how to do it*'. The last point can be important. How many good ideas are never implemented because people are not sure how to go about it? This is especially true of anything that has about it some genuine difficulty. To paraphrase G.K. Chesterton, who was writing about the decline of Christianity, it is not that some solutions are tried and found wanting, it is that they are found difficult and therefore not tried.

7. I accept

The entire thinking process outlined above will only conclude positively if the process itself has been allowed, indeed encouraged, to proceed in this manner and sequence. What is set out here is what people *like* to do, to some extent it is what their inherent reaction is to do. If it is going to happen then we have to work with it and use it to advantage.

Now remembering all this, one of the dangers is at once apparent. This is that the other person's point of view can be neglected, or ignored, with the presenter focusing primarily, or only, on their own point of view. You should ensure that you do not become introspective, concerned with your own views or situation. Instead, use and display enough empathy to come over as being constantly concerned about others' views. This sounds obvious, but it is all too easy to find your own perspective predominating, thus creating a dilution of effectiveness. Even the most important message has to earn a hearing, and this is achieved primarily through concentrating on what is important to the group. Nervousness of the actual process of presenting may compound this potential danger.

Next we turn to the structure of the presentation itself, and review how one goes through it. Probably the most famous of all maxims about any kind of communication is the old saying *'Tell'em, tell'em and tell'em'*. This can be stated more clearly as meaning that you should tell people what you are going to tell them, tell them and then tell them what it was you told them. This sounds silly, perhaps, but compare it with something a little different, the way a good report is set out, for instance.

There is an introduction, which says what it is that follows; there is the main body of the document, which goes progressively through the message; and the summary which summarises or says what has been covered. The idea is straightforward, but if it is ignored, messages may then go largely to waste.

So practising to some degree what I preach, we now split the presentation into three sections, and look at not only how to make each effective, but how to ensure that the three together make a satisfactory whole.

Structuring the presentation

Having said there are three stages – which we review under the more businesslike headings of the beginning, the middle and the end. Having said that, we start with another factor (one which is either confusing or an example of an intriguing opening!) In any case, it has been referred to before – preparation. It is that which creates your beginning, middle and end and everything else along the way.

Here I wish unashamedly to emphasise the point. Preparation is important; as Mark Twain once said, '*It usually takes me three weeks to prepare a good impromptu speech.*' If he was half as good a speaker as he was a writer it makes a point. So before we analyse a presentation, we need to think about how you put it together.

Preparation

Rarely, if ever, will you be asked just to 'talk about' something. The most crucial question any intending presenter can ask themselves is simply:

Why is this presentation to be made?

If you can answer that clearly, it will be easier both to prepare and present. Let us be clear here:

◆ Objectives are not what you intend to say, they reflect what you intend to achieve.

Forgive me if this seems obvious, but I regularly observe presentations (often carefully prepared and brought to training workshops in the knowledge that they will be subject to critique) which are poor almost solely because they have no clear objectives. They rattle along reasonably well; but they do not *actually go* anywhere.

Objectives need not only to be clear, but spelt out in sufficient detail (certainly in your own mind and sometimes for others). They must be a genuine guide to what you will do. They also need to reflect not just what you want, but the audience's view also.

Often a much-quoted acronym can provide a good guide here: **SMART**. This stands for:

Specific
Measurable
Achievable
Realistic, and
Timed.

As an example you might regard objectives linked to your reading of this book:

◆ To enable you to ensure certain of your presentations come over in future in a way that audiences will see as appropriate and informative (*specific*).

◆ To ensure (*measurable*) action takes place afterwards (here you might link to any appropriate measure: from agreements or actions that group members take, or commit to, to the volume of applause received at the end!).

◆ To be right for you: sufficient, understandable, information in manageable form that really allows you to change and improve what you do later (an *achievable* result).

◆ To also be *realistic*, that is desirable – hence a short book of short sections, (if it took you several days to read the effort might prove greater than any benefit coming from doing so).

◆ And *timed;* always a good factor to include in any objective – by when are you going to finish reading this book? When is your next presentation? How far ahead of it should you prepare?

So, ask yourself whether you are clear in this respect before you even begin to prepare. If you know *why* the presentation must be made, and *what* you intend to *achieve* then you are well on the way to success. Time spent sorting this, and making sure you have a clear vision of what the objectives are, is time well spent. It may take a few moments, but is still worth doing. Or it may need more thought and take more time. It is still worth doing, and it may well save time on later stages of preparation.

With your purpose clear, and a constant eye, as it were, on the audience, you can begin to assemble your message.

Deciding presentation content

There is more to this than simply banging down the points in sequence. A more systematic approach is necessary, indeed a more systematic approach can quickly become a habit of preparing in a way that promptly and certainly enables you to deliver what you want.

The following provides a full description of a tried and tested approach. This describes the fullest degree of preparation necessary, but it is important to stress that this is not offered as something that must be followed slavishly. The important thing is to find, experiment with, and refine and then use a method that suits *you*. In addition, practice and experience, or other factors such as familiarity with your chosen topic, may well allow you to adopt a 'shorthand' version of these approaches which is quicker, but is still effective.

It is not only necessary to **engage the brain before the mouth**, but vital to think through – in advance – what a presentation must and must not contain. The following process of thinking through and preparation is recommended solely by its practicality and can be adapted to cope with any sort of presentation, of any length or complexity and for any purpose. There are occasions when the brevity of something means this kind of approach can be reduced dramatically, and all you ultimately need is half a dozen words on cards. I am not advocating any over-engineering, but the logical thinking described here should always be in evidence.

There are five stages:

Stage 1: listing
Do not start by writing **Good morning** at the top of a page and trying to think what to say next. Forget about everything such as sequence, structure and arrangement; just concentrate on and list – in short note (or keyword) form – every significant point that the presentation

might usefully contain. Give yourself plenty of space (something larger than the standard A4 sheet is often useful: it lets you see everything at one glance). Set down the points as they occur to you, almost at random across the page. For something simple this might result only in a dozen words, or it might be far more.

You will find that this (akin to what some call 'mind-mapping') is a good thought prompter. It enables you to fill out the picture as one thought leads to another, with the freestyle approach removing the need to pause and try to link points or worry about sequence. With this done, and with some presentations it may only take a short time, you can move on to the second stage.

Stage 2: sorting

Now, you can review what you have noted down and begin to bring some order to it, deciding:

– what comes first, second and so on
– what logically links together, and how
– what provides evidence, example or illustration to the
  points.

At the same time, you can, and probably will, add some things and have second thoughts about other items which you will delete. You need to bear in mind here what kind of length is indicated and what will be acceptable.

This stage can often be completed in a short time by simply annotating and amending the first stage document. Using a second colour makes this quick and easy, as do link lines, arrows and other enhancements to the original notes.

At the same time you can begin to catch any more detailed element that comes to mind as you go through (including ways of presenting as well as what you will say), noting what it is at more length on the page or alongside.

Stage 3: arranging

Sometimes, at the end of stage two, you have a note that is sufficiently clear and from which you can work direct in preparing speaker's notes and finalising matters. If it can benefit from clarification, however, it may be worth rewriting it as a neat list; or this could be the stage where you type it and put it on a computer screen if you are working that way and want to be able to print something in due course.

Final revision is possible as you do this. Certainly you should be left with a list reflecting the content, emphasis, level of detail and so on that you feel is appropriate. You may well find you are pruning a bit to make things more manageable at this stage, rather than searching for more content and additional points to make.

Stage 4: reviewing

This may be unnecessary. Sufficient thought may have been brought to bear through earlier stages. However, for something particularly complex or important (or both), it may be worth running a final rule over what you now have written down. Sleep on it first perhaps, or check with a colleague – **Is there anything else I should include?** Certainly avoid finalising matters for a moment if you have got too close to it. It is easy to find you cannot see the wood for the trees.

Make any final amendments to the list (if this is on screen it is a simple matter) and use this as your final 'route map' as preparation continues.

Stage 5: draft your speaker's notes

Now you can turn your firm intentions about content into something representing not only what will be said, but also *how* you will put it over. This must be done carefully, though the earlier work will have helped to make it easier and quicker to get the necessary detail down.

A couple of tips:

◆ If possible, **choose the right moment**. There seem to be times when thoughts flow more easily than others (and it may help literally to talk it through to yourself as you go through this stage). Certainly interruptions can disrupt the flow and make the process take much longer, as you recap and restart again and again. The right time, uninterrupted time in a comfortable environment may all help

Keep going. By this I mean do not pause and agonise over one small point, a heading or some other detail. You can always come back to that, indeed it may be easier to complete later. If you keep going you maintain the flow, allowing consistent thinking to carry you through the structure to the end so that you can 'see' the overall shape. Once you have the main details then you can go back and fine tune, adding any final thoughts to complete the picture. The precise format of notes can be very helpful, something that is investigated separately.

Stage 6: a final check

A final look (perhaps after taking a break) is always valuable. This is also the time to consider rehearsal. Either talking it through to yourself, into a tape recorder or to a friend or colleague, or going through a full-scale dress rehearsal.

NOTE: if you are speaking as part of a team, *always* make sure that speakers get together ahead of the event to rehearse, or at least discuss, both any possible overlaps and any necessary handover between speakers. You are seeking to create what appears to the audience to be a seamless transition between separate contributors.

Thereafter, depending on the nature of the presentation, it may be useful or necessary to spend more time, either in revision or just reading over what you plan to do. You should not overdo revision at this stage, however, there comes a time to simply be content you have it right and stick with it.

This whole preparation process is important and not to be skimped. Preparation does get easier however. You will find that, with practice, you begin to produce material that needs less amendment and that both getting it down and the subsequent revision begin to take less time.

You need to find your own version of the procedures set out here. A systematic approach helps, but the intention is not to over-engineer the process. What matters is that you are comfortable with your chosen approach, and that it works for you. If this is the case, provided it remains consciously designed to achieve what is necessary, it will become a habit. It will need less thinking about, yet still act to guarantee that you turn out something that you are content meets the needs – whatever they may be.

The Preparation: Stage by Stage

We shall now look at the presentation stage by stage and start, with appropriate logic, at the beginning.

Stage 1: The beginning

The beginning is clearly an important stage. People are uncertain, they are saying to themselves *'what will this be like?'*, *'will I find it interesting or helpful?'*. They may also have their minds on other matters: what is going on back at the office, the job they left half finished, how will their assistant cope when they are away even for a few minutes? This is particularly true when the people in the group do not know you, or know you well. They then have little or no previous experience of what to expect, and this will condition their thinking (it is also possible that previous experience will make them wary!). With people you know well there is less of a problem, but the first moments of any speech are nevertheless always important.

The beginning is not only important to the participants, it is important to the presenter. Nothing settles the nerves – and even the most experienced speakers usually have a few qualms before they start – better than making a good start. Remember, the beginning is, necessarily, the introduction; the main objective is therefore to set the scene, state the topic (and rationale for it) clearly, and begin to discuss the 'meat' of the content. In addition, you have to gain the group's attention – they will never take the message on board if they are not concentrating and taking in what goes on – and create some sort of rapport both between you and the group, and around the group itself.

Let us take these aspects in turn.

◆ Gaining attention

This is primarily achieved by your manner and by the start you make. You have to look the part, your manner has to say *'this will be interesting'*, *'this person knows what they are talking about'*. A little has been said about such factors as appearance, standing up, and so on. Suffice it to say here that if your start appears hesitant, the wrong impression will be given and, at worst, everything thereafter will be more difficult.

More important is what you say first and how it is said. There are a number of types of opening, each presenting a range of opportunities for differing lead-ins. For example:

- **A question**: rhetorical or otherwise, preferably something that people are likely to respond to positively:

  'Would you welcome a better way to...?'

- **A quotation**: which might be humorous or make a point, which might be a classic, or novel phrase; or it might be something internal:

  'At the last company meeting, the M.D. said...'

- **A story**: again, something that makes a point, relates to the situation or people, or draws on a common memory:

'We all remember the situation at the end of the last financial year when...'

- **A factual statement**: perhaps striking, thought provoking, challenging or surprising:

'Do you realise that this company receives 120 complaints every working day?' (The fact that this is also a question indicates that different types of opening can be linked.)

- **A dramatic statement**: a story with a startling end, perhaps. Or a statement that surprises in some way:

For instance, once, talking about direct mail advertising, I started by asking the group to count, out loud and in unison from 1–10. Between two and three I banged my fist down on the table saying *'Stop!'* loudly. *'And that'*, I continued, *'is how long your direct mail has to catch people's attention – 2½ seconds!'*

- **An historical fact**: a reference back to an event which is a common experience of the group:

'In 2000, when company sales for what was then a new product were just...'

- **A curious opening**: simply a statement sufficiently odd for people to wait to find what on earth it is all about:

'Consider the aardvark, and how it shares a characteristic of some of our managers...' (In case you want a link, it is thick skinned.)

- **A checklist**: perhaps makes a good start when placing a 'shopping list' in people's minds early on is important:

   'There are 10 key stages to the process we want to discuss, first...'

There may be more methods and combinations of methods you can think of – whatever lead-in you pick, this element of the session needs careful, and perhaps very precise preparation.

◆ **Creating rapport**
   At the same time, you need to ensure that an appropriate group feeling is started. In terms of what you say (participation also has a role here), you may want to set a pattern of 'we' rather than 'them and us'; in other words, say *'we need to consider...'* and not *'you must...'*. If this approach is followed then a more comfortable atmosphere is created: you may add – discreetly – a compliment or two (*'As experienced people, you will...'*), though without exaggerating. Above all, *be enthusiastic.* It is said that the one good aspect of life that is infectious is enthusiasm so use it.

The opening stages need to make it absolutely clear what the objectives are, what will be dealt with, and how it will benefit those present. It must also move us into the topic in a constructive way.

This opening stage is the first 'Tell'em' from 'Tell'em, tell'em and tell'em', and directs itself at the first two stages of the group's thinking process.

Stage 2: The middle

The middle is the core of the session. The objectives are clear:

◆ to put over the detail of the message
◆ ensure acceptance of the message
◆ maintain attention throughout the process.

You also need to anticipate, prevent and, if necessary, handle any possible objections.

One of the principles here is to take one point at a time; we shall do just that here.

Putting over the content

The main trick here is to adopt a structured approach. Make sure you are dealing with points in a logical sequence, for instance, working through a process in a chronological order. And use what is referred to in communications literature as 'flagging' or 'signposting', that is straight back to the three 'tell'ems'. You cannot say things like — *'There are three key points here; performance, method and cost; let's deal with them in turn. First, performance...*' too much. Giving advance warning of what is coming (this applies to both content and the nature of what is being said. Saying '*For example ...*' is a simple form of signposting. It makes it clear what you are doing and also that you are not moving onto the next content point just yet). Putting everything in context, and relating it to a planned sequence keeps the message organised and improves understanding.

This technique, and the clarity it helps produce, gives you the overall effect you want. People must obviously understand what you are talking about. There is no room for verbosity, for too much jargon, or for anything which clouds understanding. One pretty good measure of the presenter is when people afterwards feel that, perhaps for the first time, they really have come to clearly understand something which has just been explained.

You cannot refer to 'manual excavation devices'; in presenting a spade has to be called a spade. What is more, it has, as it were, to be an interesting spade if it is to be referred to at all and if attention is to be maintained.

Maintaining attention
Here again the principles are straightforward.

Keep stressing the relevance of what is being discussed to the audience. For instance, do not say that some matter will be a cost saving to the organisation, stress personal benefits – will it make something easier, quicker or more satisfying to do, perhaps?

Make sure that the presentation remains visually interesting by using visual aids and demonstrations wherever possible.

Use descriptions that incorporate stories, or anecdotes to make the message live. You cannot make a presentation live by formal content alone, you need an occasional anecdote, or something else less formal. It is nice if you are able both to proceed through the content you must present and seemingly remain flexible, apparently digressing and adding in something interesting, a point that exemplifies or makes something more interesting as you go. How do you do this? It is back to preparation.

Finally, continue to generate attention through your own interest and enthusiasm.

Obtaining acceptance

People will only implement what they have come to believe is good sense. It is not enough to have put the message over and for it to be understood – it has to be *believed*.

Here we must start by going back to understanding. Nothing will be truly accepted unless this is achieved.

Note that to some extent better understanding is helped by:

◆ *Using clear, precise language* – language which is familiar to those present, and which does not over-use jargon.

◆ *Making explanation clear*, making no assumptions, using plenty of similes (you can hardly say '*this is like...*' too often), and with sufficient detail to get the point across. One danger here is that in explaining points that you know well, you start to abbreviate, allowing your understanding to blind you as to how far back it is necessary to go with people for whom the message is new.

◆ *Demonstration adds considerably to the chances of understanding.* This can be specific: talk about products, for instance, and it may be worth showing one. In this case, the golden rule is preparation. Credibility is immediately at risk if something is mentioned and needs visualising, yet cannot be. Help your audience's imagination and your message will go over better.

◆ *Visual aids are a powerful aid to understanding.* As the old saying has it, 'a picture is worth a thousand words'; graphs are an excellent example of this. Many people instantly understand a point illustrated by a clear graph that might well elude them in a mass of figures. (Visual aids are commented on in Chapter 3.)

Effectiveness is not, however, just a question of under-standing. As has been said, acceptance is also vital. Acceptance is helped by factors already mentioned (telling people how something will benefit them – or others they are concerned about, such as their staff). The more specific this link can be made the better the effect will be on the view formed.

In addition, acceptance may only come once credibility has been established, and this, in turn, may demand something other than your saying, in effect, *'this is right'*. Credibility can be improved by such things as references and things other people say. A description that shows how well an idea or system has worked in another department, and sets this out clearly, may be a powerful argument. References are always dependent on the source of the reference being respected. If the other department is regarded in a negative way, then their adopting some process or product may be regarded by others as being a very good reason *not* to have anything to do with it. References work best when the results of what is being quoted are included so that the message says they did this and so and so has occurred since, with sufficient details to make it interesting and credible.

Finally, it is worth making the point that you will not always know whether acceptance of a point has been achieved, unless you check. People cannot be expected to nod or speak out at every point, yet knowing that you have achieved acceptance may be important as you proceed. Questions to establish appropriate feedback are therefore a necessary part of this process, and in some presentations this must be done as you progress. It is also advisable to keep an eye on the visible signs, watching, for instance, for puzzled looks.

Handling objections

The first aspect here is the anticipation, indeed the pre-emption, of objections. On occasions it is clear that some subject to be dealt with is likely, even guaranteed, to produce a negative reaction. If there is a clear answer then it can be built into the presentation, avoiding any waste of time. It may be as simple as a comment such as *'Of course, this needs time, always a scarce resource, but once set up is done time will be regularly saved'*, which then goes on to explain how this will happen.

Otherwise, if objections are voiced – and of course on occasion they will be – then a systematic procedure is necessary if they are to be dealt with smoothly.

First, give it a moment: too glib an answer may be mistrusted or make the questioner feel – or look – silly. So, pause and for long enough to give yourself time to think (which you might just need!), and give the impression of consideration. An acknowledgement reinforces this: '*That's a good point*', '*We must certainly think about that*', though be careful of letting such a comment become a reflex and being seen as such. Then you can answer, with either a concentration on the individual's point and perspective, or with a general emphasis which is more useful to the group as a whole; or both in turn.

Very importantly, never bluff. If you do not know the answer you must say so (no group expects you to be infallible), though you may well have to find out the answer later and report back. Alternatively, does anyone else know? Similarly, even when you can answer, there is no harm in delaying a reply: '*That's a good point, perhaps I can pick it up, in context, when we deal with . . .*'.

A final word here: beware of digression. It is good to answer any ancillary points that come up, but you can stray too far. Part of the presenter's job is that of chairperson; everything planned for the session has to be covered, and before the scheduled finishing time. If therefore, you have to draw a close to a line of enquiry, and you may well have to do so, make it clear that time is pressing. Do not ever let anyone feel it was a silly point to raise.

After all this, when we have been through the session, the time comes to close.

Stage 3: The end

Always end on a high note. The group expect it, if only subconsciously. It is an opportunity to build on past success during the session or, occasionally, to make amends for anything that has been less successful.

The end is a pulling together of the overall message of the presentation. However you finally end, there is often a need to summarise in an orderly fashion. This may well be linked to an action plan for the future, so that what has been said is reviewed (completing the 'tell'ems') and a commitment is sought about what should happen next. This is important. Most people are under pressure for time and, whatever else, you have already taken up some of that. They will be busier after even half an hour taken to sit through your presentation than would be the case if they had not attended, so there is a real temptation to put everything on one side and get back to work. Yet this may be just where a little time needs to be put in to start to make some changes. Their having a real intention in mind as they leave the session is not a guarantee that action will flow, but it is a start. It makes it that much more likely that something will happen, especially if follow up action is taken to remind them and see the matter through.

Like the beginning, there is then a need to find a way of handling the final signing off. You can, for instance, finish with:

◆ *A question*: that leaves the final message hanging in the air, or makes it more likely that people will go on thinking about the issues a little longer:

'*I asked a question at the start of the session, now let us finish with another . . .*'.

◆ *A quotation* that encapsulates an important, or the last, point:

'*Good communication is as stimulating as black coffee, and just as hard to sleep after*' (Anne Morrow Lindberg).

Alternatively, choose something that, while not linked inextricably to the topic, just makes a good closing line, for example:

'*The more I practise, the more good luck I seem to have*' (which is attributed to just about every famous golfer there is), is one that might suit something with a training or instructional content.

◆ *A story*: longer than a quotation, but with the same sort of intention. If it is meant to amuse, be sure it does; you have no further chance at the end to retrieve the situation. I will resist the temptation to given an example, though a story-type close does not only imply a humorous one.

◆ *An alternative*: this may be as simple as '*Will you do this or not?*', or the more complicated option of a spelt out plan A, B, or C.

◆ *Immediate gain*: this is an injunction to act linked to an advantage of doing so now.

'*Put this new system in place and you will be saving time and money tomorrow*'. More fiercely phrased, it is called a fear based end: '*Unless you ensure this system is running you will not . . .*'. Although there is sometimes a place for the latter, the positive route is usually better.

However you decide to wrap things up, the end should be a logical conclusion, rather than something separate added to the end.

All of this is common to any presentation. The importance of presentations vary, however. Some have more complex objectives than others; in simple terms you may want to inform, motivate, persuade, change attitudes, demonstrate, prompt action and more. Sometimes several of these are grouped together.

Consider an example. You want people to understand and take on board doing something differently. You want people not just to say that they understood the presentation and perhaps even enjoyed it, you want them to have learnt from it. The ways in which people learn are therefore important principles to keep in mind throughout. It needs patience as well as intellectual weight or 'clout'. It needs sensitivity to the feedback as well as the ability to come through it. As with many skills, the difficulty is less with the individual elements, most of which are straightforward and common sense, than with the orchestration of the whole process. Many people in business must be able to present effectively, to remain flexible throughout, and work with an audience rather than just talking at them.

Whatever it is you do – *you make it happen*. Thus you must *plan to make it happen*. You can rarely, if ever, 'just wing it', it needs care in preparation and in execution. Given appropriate consideration you can make it go well. The next section sets out guidelines for some typical situations to act both as examples to illustrate the principles and as a planning aid to undertaking specific presentational tasks. First, in two further short chapters in this section are some details about using visual aids and speaker's notes.

CHAPTER 2

Speaker's Notes

For most people having *something* in front of them as they speak is essential. The question is what form exactly should it take? Speaker's notes have several roles:

◆ To boost confidence: in the event you may not need everything that is in front of you, but knowing it is there is useful.

◆ To act as a guide to what you will say and in what order.

◆ To assist you to say it in the best possible way: producing the right variety, pace, emphasis etc. as you go along.

On the other hand your notes must not act as a straightjacket and stifle all possibility of flexibility. After all, what happens if your audience's interest suggests a digression or the need for more detail before proceeding? Or the reverse, if a greater level of prior information or experience becomes apparent, meaning that you want to recast or abbreviate something you plan to say? Or if, as you get up to speak for half an hour, the person in the Chair whispers *'Can you keep it to twenty minutes? We are running a bit behind'*. Good notes should assist with these and other scenarios as well.

Again there is no intention here either to be comprehensive or to suggest only one way makes sense. Rather I will set out what seem to me some rules and some tried and tested approaches. But the intention is not to suggest that you follow what is here slavishly. Again it is important to find what suits you, so you may want to try some of the approaches mentioned, but to amend or tailor them to suit your kind of presentation as exactly as possible.

One point is worth making at the outset, there is advantage in adopting (if not immediately) a consistent approach to how you work here. This can act to make preparation more certain and you are more likely also to become quicker and quicker at getting your preparation done if you do so.

Rules for good speaker's notes

The following might be adopted as **rules**:

◆ **Legibility is essential** (you must use a sufficiently large typeface, or writing. Avoid adding tiny, untidy embellishments and remember that notes must be suitable to be used standing up and therefore at a greater distance from your eyes than if you sat to read them.)

◆ **The materials must be well chosen – for you**. Some people favour small cards, others larger sheets. A standard A4 ring binder works well (one with a pocket at the front may be useful for ancillary items you may want with you). Whatever you choose, make sure it *lies flat*. It is certain to be disconcerting if a folded page turns back on itself – especially if you repeat a whole section as I once saw happen (I can still vividly remember the moment when the speaker realised, somewhat late, what they were doing – sheer Schadenfreude).

◆ **Use only one side of the paper.** This allows space for amendment and addition if necessary and/or makes the total package easier to follow (some people like notes arranged with slides reproduced alongside to produce a comprehensive double-page spread).

◆ **Always page number your material** (yes, one day, as sure as the sun rises in the morning, you will drop it) – some people like to number the pages in reverse order – 10, 9, 8 etc. – which gives some guidance regarding time remaining until the end. Decide on one method – and stick to it to avoid confusion.

◆ **Separate different types of note**: for example *what you intend to say* and *how* (emphasis etc).

◆ **Use colour and symbols** to help you find your way, yet minimise what must be noted.

Never put down verbatim what you want to say. Reading something is difficult and always sounds less than 'fresh'. The detail on the speaker's notes needs to be just sufficient for a well-prepared speaker to be able to work from it comfortably. Consider the devices mentioned here, and try to bear in mind as you do so the effect that the use of a second, or third colour (which cannot be reproduced here) would have on its ease of use. Some highlighting is clearly more dramatic in fluorescent yellow, for example.

Back to the ideas: there should be things here you can copy or adapt, or which prompt additional ideas that suit you.

Main divisions – the pages – imagine they are A4 – are divided (a coloured line is best) into smaller segments, each creating a manageable area on which the eye can focus with ease. This helps ensure that you do not lose your place (effectively it produces something of the effect of using cards rather than sheets).

Symbols – save space and visually jump off the page making sure you do not miss them. It is best to avoid possible confusion by always using the same symbol to represent the same thing – and maybe also to restrict the overall number used; a plethora of them might become difficult to follow. Bold explanation marks and **S1** etc. to show which slide is shown where, are examples.

Columns – these separate different elements of the notes. Clearly there are various options here in terms of numbers of columns and what goes where.

Space – turning over only takes a second (often you can end a page where a slight pause is necessary anyway). It is always best to give yourself plenty of space, not least to facilitate amendments and, of course, to allow individual elements to stand out.

Emphasis – this must be as clear as content; again a second colour helps.

Timing – an indication of time elapsed (or still to go) can be included as little or often as you find useful. Remember the audience love to have time commitments kept.

Options – this term is used to describe points included as a separate element and can be particularly useful. Options can be added or omitted depending on such factors as time and feedback. They help fine tune the final delivery – and are also good for confidence. They might go in a third right-hand column.

Note: Points in the 'Options' column are designed to be included or not depending on the situation. A plan might therefore include ten points under options, with half of them (regardless of which) making your total presentation up to the planned duration. So you can extend or decrease to order and fluently work in additional material where more detail (or an aside or example) seems appropriate on the day.

Good preparation and good notes go together. If you are well prepared, confident of your material and confident also that you have a really clear guide in front of you, then you are well on the way to making a good presentation.

A suggestion of the sort of planning sheet that might be helpful follows on page 49. This is designed to act as both a checklist and a way of setting out your first thoughts.

PRESENTATION PLANNER

Topic or title:

Duration (specified or estimated):

My intentions are to:

My overall objective can be summed up as:

Summary of main points to be made:

STRUCTURE

The logic and sequence used will be:

The Beginning

Things to make clear:

Content:

The Middle

The End

Final 'sign-off'

Additional points:

CHAPTER 3

Visual Aids

Perhaps the most important visual aid has already been mentioned: it is you. Numbers of factors, such as simple gestures (for example, a hand pointing), and more dramatic ones like banging a fist on the table, which I like to describe as flourishes, are part of this, as is your general manner and appearance.

More tangible forms of visual aid are also important. Such things as slides serve several roles, including:

◆ focusing attention within the group
◆ helping change pace, add variety etc.
◆ giving a visual aspect to something
◆ acting as signposts to where within the structure the presentation has reached.

They also help the presenter, providing reminders over and above the speaker's notes on what comes next.

Be careful. Visual aids should *support* the message, not lead or take it over. Just because slides exist or are easy to originate does not mean they will be right. You need to start by looking at the message, at what you are trying to do, and see what will help put it over and have an additive effect. They may make a point that is difficult or impossible to describe, in the way a graph might make a point instantly which would be lost in a mass of figures.

Or you may have a particular reason to use them; to help get a large amount of information over more quickly, perhaps.

The checklist that follows deals briefly with the various options, offers general guidance on visuals production, and some tips on using the ubiquitous OHP (overhead projector) and PowerPoint:

General principles of using visual aids

◆ Keep the content simple.

◆ Restrict the amount of information and the number of words:
  − use single words to give structure, headings, or short statements
  − avoid it looking cluttered or complicated
  − use a running logo (e.g. the main heading/ topic on each slide).

◆ Use diagrams, graphs etc where possible rather than too many figures; and never read figures aloud without visual support.

◆ Build in variety within the overall theme, for example, with colour or variations of the form of aid used.

◆ Emphasise the theme and structure, for example, regularly using a single aid to recap the agenda or objectives

◆ Ensure the content of the visual matches the words.

◆ Make sure content is necessary and relevant.

◆ Ensure everything is visible. Ask yourself: is it clear? will it work in the room? does it suit the equipment? (Colours, and the right sized typeface help here.)

◆ Ensure the layout emphasises the meaning you want (and not some minor detail).

◆ Pick the right aid for the right purpose.

Using an OHP (overhead projector)

Some care should be taken in using an overhead projector to begin with; they appear deceptively simple, but present inherent hazards to the unwary. The following hints may well be useful:

◆ Make sure the electric flex is out of the way (or taped to the floor); falling over it will improve neither your presentation nor your dignity.

◆ Make sure it works before you start using it with the group (this goes for the second bulb – and a spare, even – and the roll of acetate film if you are using one).

◆ Make sure it is positioned where you want it within reach, and gives you room to move and has space alongside for papers. (*Note:* it may need to be in a slightly different place for left/right handed people – a hazard for some team presentations.)

◆ Stand back and to the side of it: be sure not to obscure the view of the screen for anyone in the group.

◆ Having made sure the picture is in focus, look primarily at the machine and not the screen – the OHP's primary advantage is to keep you facing the front.

◆ Only use slides that have large typefaces or images and, if you plan to write on acetate, check how large your handwriting needs to be.

◆ Switch off when changing slides; it looks more professional than the jumbled image that appears as slides are changed while the unit is switched on.

◆ If you want to project the image on a slide progressively you can cover the bottom part of the image with a sheet on paper (on the machine). Use paper that is not too thick and you can still see the whole image through it even though the whole image is not projected. As you slide the paper down it may be useful to put a weight on it, otherwise it reaches the point where it must be held or will drop off.

◆ For handwritten use an acetate roll (fitted running from the back to the front of the machine) minimises the amount of acetate used (it is expensive) and removes the need to keep changing loose sheets.

◆ Remember that when something new is shown, all attention is, at least momentarily, on it – pause, or what you say may be missed.

◆ It may be useful to add emphasis by highlighting certain things on the slides as you go through them. If you slip the slide *under* the acetate roll you can do this without adjustment and without marking the slide.

◆ Similarly, two slides shown together can add information (or you can use overlays attached to the slide and folded across). Alternatively, the second slide may have minimal information on it, with such things as a title talk, session heading, or company logo remaining in view on one as others are shown by being placed over it.

◆ If you want to point something out and highlight it, then this is most easily done by laying a small pointer (or pencil) on the projector. Extending pointers are, in my view, almost impossible to use without appearing pretentious, and they risk you turning your back on the group unnecessarily.

PowerPoint

This (and, to be fair, other systems) allows you to prepare slides on your computer and project them through a projector using the computer to control the show. So far so good. It works well and you have the ability to use a variety of layouts, colours, illustrations and so on at the touch of a button.

The dangers

There are some dangers (and many of the points made in reviewing the use of an OHP apply equally here). First, do not let the technology carry you away. Not everything it will do is useful – certainly not all on one slide or even in one presentation – and it is a common error to allow the ease of preparation to increase the amount on a slide beyond the point where it becomes cluttered and difficult to follow. This might also lead you to use too many slides. Similarly, if you are going to use its various features, like the ability to strip in one line and then another to make up a full picture, remember to keep it manageable. Details here can be important, for instance colour choice is prodigious but not all are equally suitable for making things clear.

The second danger is simply the increased risk of technological complexity. Sometimes it is a simple error. Recently I saw an important presentation have to proceed without the planned slides because the projector (resident at the venue) could not be connected to the laptop computer (which had been brought to the venue) because the leads were incompatible. Sometimes problems may be caused by something buried in the software. Again not long ago I sat through a presentation that used twenty or thirty slides. Each time the slide was changed there was an unplanned delay of three or four seconds. It was felt unwarranted to stop and risk tinkering with the equipment, but long before the three-quarters of an hour presentation finished everyone in the group found it disproportionately maddening.

So make sure (check, check, check . . .) that everything is going to work. Run off transparencies that can be shown on an OHP if, in the event of disaster striking, this would be a sensible insurance (or a paper handout copy). Finally follow all the overall rules and do not forget that you do not have to have a slide on all the time – when you have finished with one blank out the screen until you are ready for the next.

Whatever you use, remember to talk to the group not to the visual aid. Looking at the screen too much when slides are used is a common fault. Make sure visuals are visible (do not get in the way yourself), explain them or their purpose as necessary, mention whether or not people will get a paper copy of them and stop them distracting by removing them as soon as you are finished with them.

Beware gremlins

Is it one of Murphy's Laws? Certainly it is an accurate maxim that if something can go wrong it will; and nowhere is this more true than with equipment.

The moral: check, check and check again. Everything – from the spare OHP bulb (do not even think about using an old machine with only one bulb) to which way up 35mm slides are going to be, even whether the pens for the flipchart still work – is worth checking.

Always double-check anything with which you are unfamiliar, especially if, like with a microphone for instance, what you do is going to be significantly dependent on it. And remember that while the sophistication of equipment increases all the time, so too do the number of things that can potentially go wrong.

The concept of contingency is worth a thought; what do you do if disaster does strike? You have been warned.

Being inventive

Finally, be inventive. Practically anything can act as a visual aid, from another person (carefully briefed to play their part) to an exhibit of some sort. In a business presentation, exhibits may be obvious items: products, samples, posters etc or maybe something totally unexpected.

Externally there are hotels and conference centres whose proud boast is that access and strength allow you to say: *What we need now is some really heavyweight support* - as the baby elephant actually walks across the platform behind you. The possibilities are virtually endless.

Like all the skills involved in making presentations, while the basics give you a sound foundation, the process is something that can benefit from a little imagination.

PART TWO
MANAGEMENT TOPICS

Introduction

In this section of the book, guidelines are given on how to tackle twenty-four selected typical speaking tasks. These are designed to:

♦ Specifically assist you in preparing and undertaking these particular assignments.

♦ Act as examples, providing information useful to undertaking something essentially similar to the examples.

♦ Provide a further review and information about the whole process, in other words to pick up and say something about techniques and approaches which are both important to a particular task, and which also have more general application.

The examples are chosen to be representative of the kind of thing most managers may have to do; some topics will remind you of others which need a broadly similar approach. All may make points that can help in wider situations.

In every case, whatever speaking task you may face, it is helpful to ensure you are absolutely clear why the task is necessary – what the objectives are – and to think through systematically what needs to be said and how.

After a few introductory remarks, each entry is arranged under the same headings:

Maximising the opportunity
Key things to include
Dangers to avoid
Creating a clear structure
Beginning
Middle
End
Overall
Additional dimensions
Visual aids
Duration
Speaker's notes
Useful quotes

The intention is not to provide a complete blueprint, so the principles set out in the book's Introduction are not constantly repeated, rather those elements that are especially important with regard to an individual topic are highlighted. In the few minutes that it takes to read the comments on a particular topic, you can pick up pointers and stimulate your own thinking prior to preparing something you have to undertake.

Giving Congratulations

Here is an occasion that you *want* to occur regularly. It might follow any sort of success: a project successfully completed, a large sales order, a promotion, an extra effort. Success might relate to a routine matter or to something really exceptional. It might be one small part of what goes on or itself have a disproportional effect on operations.

The success might have been achieved by an individual or by a group of people; whoever has done what – you decide to tell them it was appreciated.

Maximising the opportunity

The immediate opportunity is to make the successful person (or people) feel good. This is clear 'recognition of achievement', straight out of motivation theory, and the objective is to improve their morale. But, as so often is the case, there may be more to bear in mind. Such as:

◆ encouraging repeat action or still greater efforts

◆ encouraging others to act likewise

◆ explaining just how important such action is and how it helps

◆ making up for past difficulties

◆ acknowledging the specific nature of the

achievement (perhaps it was done in adverse circumstances).

In addition, you may want to come over as caring, appreciative and impressed. This represents a good opportunity and one worth getting just right if it is to work hard for you.

Key things to include

Unequivocal praise (if not, why are you saying anything at all?).

A clear statement, or explanation, of what was done, if necessary how and in what circumstances and – often the most important thing – what results accrued. You may want to build it up for others present, or to link the specific result to more general points.

If you are going to mention other things, make the link clear and do not let anything appear to belittle the core congratulations.

Last, a small point, but with anything so personal, get people's names right!

Dangers to avoid

The key thing is *not* on any account to sound patronising. If it is thought you are *just saying something because you have to,* its value will not be lessened – it will be nil. Avoiding this is largely achieved through manner, tone of voice and choice of words. Even uncertainty about what to say (because you are attempting to wing it) may come across as uncaring. Similarly, do not be vague, calling something *quite good* when it needs more of a superlative, as this will just dilute its impact.

The second main danger is to bury the congratulations, by giving other things too much emphasis or time, and apparently belittling it.

Conversely, be careful too not to make the occasion sound too brief and informal if you want to use it to make serious points more broadly.

Creating clear structure

Beginning

◆ Make it very clear right at the start that congratulations are in order: *Right, let's be clear, I want to say an enormous 'thank you' to Mary. Some of us may not understand just what a success she has had, . . .*

◆ Only then state the nature of your speech (e.g. just a thank you, or something more – encapsulating what it will be in just a few words).

Middle

◆ Remain organised throughout.

◆ Do not say too much, and keep any separate elements of the content well balanced.

- Separate elements must be explained and put succinctly so as to be accepted.

- Remember one useful rule about humour, and *never* say anything that will personally embarrass someone. This will rather negate the motivational nature of the occasion.

End

Always finish at the heart of your theme by repeating your congratulations and thanks. And link to anything that follows (for example, food and drink, which might be announced by a toast). A light or humorous touch at the end may well suit.

Overall

- Be sure to find some good phrases. Just *Thank you,* may be insufficient. *A very good result* sounds bland and therefore risks not conveying much meaning. If you mean *What a result! Unexpected – even by Mary – first class and more than any would have dared to hope – well done you, it's something we will all remember for a long time,* then say so.

- In terms of manner, this needs to be done enthusiastically and with something of a feel of spontaneity. To achieve this you must prepare sufficiently thoroughly so as to become familiar with your intentions. You will then not have to follow every tiny detail of your notes, which can suppress the feeling of spontaneity.

Additional dimensions

◆ A chance to reply? Maybe in a speech replying or just by allowing an informal word or two: *It was a great result – what did you think when you heard, Mary?* Equally you may want to protect someone from cries of *Speech!*

◆ Manage anything you have to cope with physically carefully (and think about it beforehand). If you need to produce a bunch of flowers with a flourish think about where it sits meantime – somewhere safe and secret.

Visual aids

◆ Slides of any sort are not likely to be right.

◆ Something to show might add to your manner (e.g. the award if there is one, or just waving the report announcing results enthusiastically might be enough).

Duration

Not too long for this sort of thing, and flag time in advance – *I'd like to take three or four minutes to . . .*

Watch the balance of time between the main message and any other elements.

Speaker's notes

Probably brief, perhaps a postcard or two.

Useful quotes

'The only place where success comes before work is in the dictionary.' *Vidal Sassoon*

'Some people pay a compliment as if they expected a receipt.' *Kin Hubbard*

'I can live for two months on a good compliment.' *Mark Twain*

'What really flatters a man is that you think him worth flattering.' *George Bernard Shaw*

Issuing a reprimand

Sometimes people do wrong. It may occur for various reasons from slight inattention to Machiavellian destructiveness; and sometimes something needs to be said about it publicly. Keep two things separate here. An individual is normally most appropriately dealt with in a one-to-one situation, but it may separately be necessary to address a group or team about some transgression in which they are all involved.

Perhaps the first thing to resolve is that this is something to be approached, and described, constructively. A session that ends up seeming just to 'have a go' at people may achieve little. As well as what you do *not* want done, you need to think about any change you aim to instigate.

Maximising the opportunity

The prime opportunity here is not in recriminations, but in influencing the future. You need to keep a clear perspective on the matter, it might be easy to allow, say, anger at something that has happened predominate and obscure specific things that such a speech might achieve. These could include:

◆ making clear the implications of the error

◆ explaining, if necessary, how the error occurred

◆ setting out *what* needs to be done to prevent a reccurrence

◆ setting out *how* such action can be completed

◆ motivating people to ensure they *want* to adapt their behaviour

◆ linking to any systems and controls involved

◆ linking also to any exceptional, perhaps temporary, measures to be put in place to monitor the situation.

You may want to make the seriousness of the matter clear and do so in a firm manner, but the main emphasis of the session must surely look to the future – and do so constructively.

Key things to include

A clear statement of what happened (and its significance) that is factually correct and which does not exaggerate .

A description of people's responsibilities; this might be a light recap or need to go back to basics to a greater extent.

An explanation of the importance of the area under review (it will help if this can be couched in terms of the individuals as well as the organisation).

Clear instructions about what should be done in future, and a clear distinction between what was previously the case and any new, revised or additional instructions that are now to be put in place.

Dangers to avoid

Do not lose your temper (however much you feel this is justified), a rant will not put things right in the way that a considered and measured response will. You may elect to display a measure or disappointment or anger, but it should be well controlled.

Put what is being said in proper context, it must not be seen as a general moan.

Take action promptly, if facts are disputed just because no-one now remembers exactly what happened this will not help make the session constructive.

Do not let the session deteriorate into a slanging match (if some participation is necessary then your Chairing skills must be well deployed).

Create and maintain an overall constructive feel to what is said, together with a focus on the future; the reverse of this will certainly dilute the good you can achieve.

Creating a clear structure

Beginning

◆ Make the tone you are adopting clear right at the start: disappointed, serious yet with a constructive focus on getting things right in future.

◆ A firm, straight talking feel will probably be best; start as you mean to go on.

Middle

◆ Normal organisation and a logical approach is as important as ever – take particular care to separate analysis and discussion of the *past* and intention and action for the *future*.

End

◆ Refer, if necessary, to the difficulty first as you wrap up, and end on a positive note linked to getting things right in future.

Overall

◆ The need here is to be specific. Do not say, *This could have led to a major disaster*, rather say what would have happened: *This could have stopped production for a whole day.*

◆ If this is an exceptional event (as it should be) then this may be worth saying and you might consider building in some good news along with the bad: *This was disappointing, especially in a week when we had record sales, so let's make sure that lessons are learnt and that next time...*

◆ In terms of manner, this needs treating seriously and must come over with weight and authority. It must also seem well considered and logical.

Additional dimensions

◆ In serious situations it may be necessary to anticipate a worse scenario. What happens if this, or something similar – or worse, happens again? Hinting at graver repercussions in such circumstances might be used to put this session in context and be sure it is seen as an appropriate response.

Visual aids

◆ The topic will tend to dictate what, if anything, is necessary (for example, do you need to set out figures clearly?).

◆ The brevity suggests nothing elaborate, though a checklist of planned action may be useful – this could be either a slide or a handout; or both.

Duration

Not too long, though time must allow everything to be made clear. It must not seem that you are 'dragging the thing out' inappropriately. There is something of the short, sharp shock about such a circumstance.

Speaker's notes

Nothing elaborate should be necessary, especially if the duration is not too long, but facts are important and you will need these unequivocally set out in front of you; take particular care over dates, times and other measures.

Useful quotes

'He (Napoleon) learned from the mistakes of the past how to make new ones.'   *A. J. P. Taylor*

'Experience is the name everyone gives to their mistakes.'   *Oscar Wilde*

'Smart people make mistakes. But dumb people make the same mistakes over and over again.' *Anon*

Highlighting a threat

Threats come in all sorts of guises. They may be external, from competition in the market place or government regulations. They may be internal, a cut down on costs or a 'downsizing' affecting staff numbers. They may be long anticipated or they may appear overnight and surprise everyone. Almost always they need assimilating, their effects, or likely effects, considering, and then they need a response – in the form of action. Thus an unstoppable need for cost reduction may demand that you consider different ways of doing things, competitive action may necessitate product revision or improved marketing to combat it.

The opportunity

Given the circumstances described above, there are a number of different things that may need to be done, for example to:

◆ Explain clearly *what* is happening (or predicted to happen).

◆ Explain *why* something is the case (and perhaps to make it clear no blame is involved internally).

◆ Set out – or discuss – the likely consequences.

◆ Spell out whatever action is deemed necessary and, if necessary, how that will affect people.

◆ Spell out also the degree to which this will solve the problem (some things just cannot be overturned, others may need a long campaign – in which case it needs to be explained that you are talking about phase one).

◆ Link to an action plan – who will do what and when.

◆ As ever the need to be clear and define your differing intentions may well be important.

Key things to include

Clear differentiation between the negative and the positive parts of the message; this both in terms of signposting and actual content and presentation.

Clear differentiation also between the background, current or recent circumstances and so on and the conclusions drawn and the action to follow.

Any action plan element of the messages content must be clear and not diluted by any overlap with a display of fear or resentment about the difficulty being faced.

A nice thought to keep in mind here is the way the Chinese write the word 'Crisis'. It consists two characters, the first of which means chaos and the second of which means – opportunity. Perhaps whatever the threat, it is worth trying to see if anything positive can come, or be made to come, from it.

Dangers to avoid

In the words immortalised in the television sitcom *Dad's Army – Don't panic!* The greatest danger here is acting prematurely, so that lack of clear thinking makes what should come over as a considered and practical response appear to be ill thought out or a shot in the dark.

Lack of structure, poorly chosen words or expressions or a strident note can all give the wrong impression, so although there is perhaps a feeling of desperation in the background, this must not be allowed to show and a steady hand is needed in putting your message over.

Creating a clear structure

Beginning

◆ Make it clear that the session will not all be gloom and doom, even if you have to start with the dangers.

◆ A summary of where you are going may be important and useful at the start – *Before we get into this at all, let me say that I'm confident that we can overcome the difficulty and...* (touching on the new situation to be created).

Middle

◆ A good, and well signposted, agenda.

◆ A point-by-point explanation – that keeps facts and emotions separate.

◆ A clear differentiation between the major topics of the session: for instance, the dangers, the action to be taken.

◆ A clear link to the action plan.

End

◆ There may be a good deal to be done here.
Summary may usefully touch again on the dangers
(and thus the importance of moving ahead
purposefully), but must also highlight the action
and end on an encouraging – *this is possible* – note.

Overall

◆ Do not neglect the motivational element that may
be necessary – ask yourself if you need to enthuse
people and convince them that action *will* retrieve
the situation or to put it more personally – *I am
confident that you will be able to get this done and
make this solution work.*

◆ In terms of manner, in difficult circumstances a
considered, panic-free approach will not just be
appreciated – it will give confidence.

Additional dimensions

◆ Accentuate the positive. Instead of saying *We've got
to do something about this,* rather say *We will do
something about this.*

◆ Be clear about intentions and about results. Talk
about how things will be in the future and what
effect planned action will have on the situation.

Duration

As with many topics here the complexity of the message dictates overall length. One thing you can try to organise, however, is the time spent on different elements of the message. The threat needs to be clearly described, but thereafter little time should be spent on speculation and possible ensuing disaster (though the result of inaction should be made clear) and most of the time should be spent on the action and the intended results.

Speaker's notes

Nothing special is required here, notes should reflect the structure you have selected and be sufficiently clear to allow you to give sufficient concentration to the tone and making it positive.

Useful quotes

'A man is not finished when he is defeated. He is finished when he quits.'   *Richard Nixon*

'Risk comes from not knowing what you are doing.'
      Warren Buffet

'He who stands on tiptoe does not stand firm.'
      Lao-Tzu

'There can't be a crisis this week, my diary is full.'
      Henry Kissinger

Talking about money

For any organisation money makes their world go round. It is important on both sides of the balance sheet – the only money an organisation has comes from outside itself (in a commercial one primarily from customers). Costs are important too.

There is, however, a considerable difference between what people regard as 'my money' and 'organisation money'; and the latter may somehow feel less real.

Maximising the opportunity

The purposes of discussing money may be many and varied and may indeed overlap with other topics here, for example 'mission accomplished' (see page 195). It can be for information, but may also link to action – for example if you are specifying a financial target of some sort for people, then their understanding it may be an essential preliminary to their taking action to achieve it.

So the key opportunity here is the achievement of clear understanding. This, like anything considered complex, may have a direct bearing on the way you are perceived. If you are able to get people understanding – perhaps surprised at the ease with which they are in fact appreciating something they expected to be complicated – then they like it: *I really see that now – I hadn't thought of it like that before.* This enhances the opportunity.

Key things to include

A clear spelling out of just what is going to be put over (and, as ever, why).

Sufficient background to the core content. For example, do not start talking about cost cutting without putting the need for it in context.

A careful, step-by-step approach to the detail, one that is well illustrated (see Visual aids later) and well exemplified.

And lastly, be particularly careful about checking understanding and remember that if you simply say *Everybody clear?* it takes a brave person to say that they are not.

Dangers to avoid

Pitching in too fast and without sufficient run up.

Proceeding too fast without pause for people to take in, and perhaps consider, the details.

Jumping straight to complexities, particularly if you appear to be assuming that everyone is keeping up.

Using too much jargon; with any financial terminology – sometimes even basics like *Profit and loss account*, never mind more technical phrases – it is easy to lose people quickly. Too many abbreviations such as DCF (discounted cash flow) may also dilute understanding.

Clear structure

Beginning

◆ Make sure you get attention ahead of going into any detail.

◆ If people are apprehensive about figures, say something early on to make it clear you will take care not to confuse and get them believing that they *will* understand.

Middle

◆ The key here is a logical approach with the sequence in which you are going to proceed, and the reason for it, spelt out clearly.

◆ Then a point by point progression that ensures clarity at every step along the way before going further.

◆ Make sure that the reasons for detail, and the implications of the message, are not lost in a plethora of unexplained or peripheral figures.

End

◆ Given the complexities that may be involved the key thing is to summarise the essentials, and end with a clear link between any detail that has had to be gone through and the implications and any action people in the audience must take.

Overall

◆ Always bear in mind that many people in business are not as numerate, or as quick at grasping figures, as they would like (or sometimes as they pretend!). The apocryphal story of the businessman who, asked how he made his fortune said *I started a business buying at $2 and selling at $4, and it's just amazing how that two percent mounts up* makes a point. He was able to turn a profit, but not to explain the arithmetic involved. So, never underestimate the care with which financial matters need to be explained

◆ In terms of manner, this needs the impression of concern for detail and precision of explanation. This must underlie whatever else is going on, whether it is elation about record profits or concern for excessive costs.

Additional dimensions

◆ Watch your language. It needs a particular kind of precision. For example nothing can be *About 12.3 percent*. It is either *About 12 percent* or it is specifically *12.3 percent.*

◆ Be careful to make figures relate to the people in the audience. Amounts of money that have relevance around an organisation may seem unimaginable to members of staff who may regard (say) £100 as a lot of money. For example, in one travel agency group the sum by which management sought to increase sales was a figure of hundreds of thousands of pounds. By talking about what each individual member of a branch's staff needed to do for the figure to be hit (perhaps an additional 2/3 family holidays sold each week) they made the task seem clear and manageable. This kind of amortizing is often useful; another example is saying *Less than £100 a month* instead of *£1,100*. Or vice versa; you might want to emphasise the larger sum.

Visual aids

◆ The old saying that a picture is worth a thousand words was never truer than here. Figures can very easily be confusing, so slides or visuals of some sort in a form that clarifies are a real support. Graphs are particularly useful, a pie or bar chart can provide information – accurately – and at a glance which just talk or looking at the raw figures would take much longer to impart.

◆ Beware of slides created from reports, for example columns of figures most of which you ignore and from which you extract just one or two points. Use material specifically designed to make the points you want.

Duration

Duration is not a major factor in its own right. Though rushing rather than taking time can dilute understanding. Time to make matters clear will often be appreciated. Too long without a break or a change of pace may make it difficult for those with no great facility for figures to concentrate.

Speaker's notes

As slides are likely to be important here, and may be a major part of what you need in front of you, be sure you have all the figures that you will need to quote clear and legible in front of you (watch the type size you choose if you print out material for your guidance). Organise material so that you *never* have to say *I think it was about £12,000* when it matters that it was *£11,100*.

Useful quotes

'Money is better than poverty, if only for financial reasons.'   *Woody Allen*

'Money is the only applause that a businessman gets for his performance.'   *Larry Adler*

'The two most beautiful words in the English Language? "Cheque enclosed!"'   *Dorothy Parker*

'It is not a sale until the money's in the bank.'
                                                          Overheard

---

When someone retires or leaves

Most organisations want to be seen as caring employers; so do most bosses. First you should get matters in context. We are not talking here about someone being fired, but leaving for good reasons (they might just be moving to another part of the organisation). It is unrealistic for any manager to expect that no one in their team will ever leave, or to regard it as a failure if it occurs (though it might be, so do not reject that thought). Consider what it would mean if no one ever left. The implications are negative – no one is good enough to get another job, no one has enough get up and go to have the ambition to want to move ahead. Do you want such people on your team?

So, when people do leave it is the positive elements that need to be raised in anything that is said about it.

Maximising the opportunity

There are primarily three considerations here:

◆ The motivation of the individual (and the practical side of this is that you may want to establish good long distance relations with them – for example, to be able to telephone them to clarify information from the past, or ensure they do a reasonable public relations job for the organisation or the department).

- The motivation of other people (who may one day be in the same position).

- To give attention to the gap left (maybe you want help in recruiting a replacement or changing operating procedures to allow work to be unaffected until that happens).

Key things to include

First, foremost and throughout, include some genuine thanks for what the individual has done in the past. At least some of this is best described by specific examples (and that may need some research).

A 'news' element: what are they going to be doing, when and where.

Implications: what will happen – organisationally and in terms of how things will be done – after the person has gone, though keep the focus on the immediate occasion.

If there is more to be done than speak – maybe a gift needs handing over – then build this in appropriately.

Dangers to avoid

The key thing to avoid is a feeling that what is being said is only a matter of 'form'. If people think that you subscribe to the awful American maxim that – *if you can fake the sincerity, everything else is easy,* then the occasion is doomed and will do more harm than good.

Do not let the focus drift away from the individual. For example, if significant changes will occur after the person's departure, you can hint at it or give the gist, but the details should better follow (and you can say how and when).

Probably such a session needs at least some humour. As always with this be careful not to go over the top or to embarrass people inappropriately. Perhaps too you need to make it clear what is fictitious or exaggerated rather than a genuinely true anecdote – *John has been notable not least for his style; only the other day I heard two of the secretaries discussing him. 'Doesn't John dress well,' said one, to which the other replied, 'Yes, and so quickly.'*

Clear structure

Beginning
- This may need to grab attention in an informal, or even high spirited or unruly gathering, so get straight into the session maybe in a way that suggests (carefully) that respect and courtesy for the person leaving demands silence and attention.

Middle
- Little more than a sentence can spell out what you plan to do.

- A point by point progression helps as with any talk.

- Some segregation of more or less serious points may be necessary (and certainly if you include information that is significant and needs to be noted then you should say so).

End
- ◆ Sign off on a high note, back to the thanks – the good wishes for the future – and in all likelihood a light touch as a final word.

Overall
- ◆ The other factor that affects the whole thing is the personalised nature of how you handle it; it must not, in any sense, seem like your 'standard send-off'.

- ◆ In terms of manner, the overall tone should be a positive and pleasant one (though some circumstances may tinge it with sadness – perhaps ill-health makes retirement essential though not welcomed).

Additional dimensions
- ◆ If it is appropriate for the person to say a word or two in reply, then it is sensible to tell them something about this in advance (though if the whole occasion is to be a surprise, you have no choice but to spring it on them – in which case consider how you do it, for example making light of it if you know the person will find it difficult).

- ◆ Consider carefully the differences inherent in doing this in your office or, as sometimes happens, in public – as at a leaving 'do' in a restaurant or bar.

Just bear in mind that other people may (will?) be listening, so it is not the occasion to slag off any aspect of the organisation – that guy at the next table is bound to be a customer!

◆ As whenever you speak at a social event, do not deceive yourself into thinking that a drink will calm your nerves, it is more likely to loosen your tongue and too much will put you on automatic pilot and on course for disaster.

Visual aids
◆ The informal nature of such an occasion almost certainly makes any kind of slide inappropriate, however there may be 'items' – a gift, something providing evidence of achievement – that can be used visually.

Duration

This is not an occasion to be overdone perhaps, or the speech part of it is not (bearing in mind that it may be part of a party of some kind). Nor should it be so perfunctory as to devalue the occasion or what is said.

Speaker's notes

Given the short duration of such a session, nothing elaborate is needed here. Make sure, however, that you have facts clearly in front of you (and that they are correct! – you do not want hecklers to correct you when you say – *During the nine years John has been here*).

Useful quotes

'Old age is like everything else. To make a success of it you have to start young.'   *Fred Astaire*

'I married him for better or worse, but not for lunch.'   *Hazel Weiss*

'The greatest pleasure in life is achieving things that people say can't be done.'   *Scott Volkers*

Producing a customer focus

It is said that marketing is too important to leave to marketing people. A 'marketing culture' within an organisation implies that everyone both understands how their role relates to customers (even if the actual link is somewhere down the line). Also that they are able and motivated to undertake their responsibilities in a way that contributes positively to customer satisfaction.

This philosophy also takes in the concept of 'internal customers', that is service to other people internally which, when well done, helps them to complete their tasks in a way that, in turn, increases external customer satisfaction.

The task here may range from the need to inform or motivate to what is effectively training in customer care skills (see box).

The essence of customer care

We all recognise good customer care when we are on the receiving end (more so bad service!). But to be sure that people operate in a way that maximises the opportunity the process needs some analysis. An elaborate review is beyond our brief here but the following encapsulates the essentials. It hangs around the mnemonic PERFECT.

Customer care should be:

Polite
Efficient
Respectful
Friendly
Enthusiastic
Cheerful
Tactful

It also should be reliable, consistent and even surprising, dealing with things in a way that is beyond the customers' expectations. Teasing out such a breakdown of what is required allows various aspects of the process to be investigated, and staff encouraged to keep an eye on how they operate in a manageable and meaningful way.

Leaving the detail of exactly how good customer care is delivered on one side, we can think about how the topic is approached in some kind of presentation.

Maximising the opportunity

There are two distinct opportunities here:

◆ The first is the creation, maintenance and ongoing improvement of standards of customer care in all respects (with internal and external customers), and in turn the improvement of sales and profits or other objectives.

◆ The second concerns the staff. Whatever kind of link a job has with the customer interface, maximising the effectiveness of that link is an important part of the job. Understanding that they can contribute in this way is positively motivational, as is being sufficiently well informed to be able to implement whatever is necessary to the required standard. Responsibility and achievement are involved here and continuing communications have an important role to play.

Key things to include

Clarity about how what you elect to say fits in with the total picture.

Unless you are to conduct a full training session, you cannot aim to be comprehensive. If so make it clear what you have selected to give priority to and why.

Real examples. Do not just *say* 'You must be polite' – make it clear *how – Always say please and thank you and use the customer's name*. If you give conversational examples it makes it easier to link ideas to practice.

Dangers to avoid

It is a basic principle in many areas of business that even the best performance can be improved; hence the ongoing drive for excellence in so many areas. This needs to be understood. If you unwittingly give the impression that this is a topic you are talking about because inadequate performance must be corrected (in which case matters need handling differently), then your presentation may be received only with resentment – and this can cloud the issue and dilute any acceptance of your message.

Be careful not to use examples in a way that seems to be scripting things. You are much more likely to want people to think about things and interpret what needs to be done in their own way – anything else is likely to sound parrot like and insincere.

Construct a clear structure

Beginning

◆ Get things in context, give an explanation of purpose and why certain elements are being concentrated on (and perhaps why others are not).

Middle

◆ Here you may need a formula for each part of your talk, for example: *The task being dealt with, what customers want, best approaches/phrases, how to make it work.* If you have several points to go through and such an approach fits them all it keeps the overall message well organised.

End

◆ The likelihood here is that you need an 'action' sign off, examples should continue right up to the end and because motivation is probably one of the intentions – end on a positive note.

Overall

◆ The empathy referred to here is the most important point overall. People do not just need to know how to deal with customers, and to understand why it is necessary and what can be gained when customer care works well. They need to feel how good it is for the customer to be on the receiving end of something really well done.

◆ In terms of manner, getting customer service right should be inherently important and the human contact it involves makes it interesting, so a natural approach to this is helpful. You should sound as if getting this right is something everyone will want; they may find it a challenge, but they will also find it satisfying.

Additional dimensions

◆ An important element here is empathy. People need to see things from the customers' point of view. It is easy not to do so, witness how inappropriately personally defensive people often get when dealing with complaints – a sort of *It's not my fault* approach when what the customer wants is just for

something to happen right. Thus examples are likely
to be important. Include talk of real customers and
get people to imagine situations where they
themselves are customers (as everyone is on
occasion), and you will bring the topic to life.

◆ If you speak about good current practice, do not
inappropriately take credit for it. So, do not say, *I
have heard people saying 'xxxx' and that's just the
sort of thing I want.* Rather say something like, *I
have heard Mary say 'xxxx', which seems a good way
to deal with it and gets a good response from
customers.*

Visual aids

◆ A standard approach is all that is required here.
Checklist slides to keep matters on track (and help
make something like the PERFECT mnemonic
memorable), and maybe some visuals to illustrate
other kinds of principle (the different attitudes
displayed by different customers, perhaps).

◆ This kind of session can be short and informative
or it can overlap into training. The more it falls
into the latter category the more likely it is that
slides will help. Additionally, staff distanced from
customers in a direct sense may need more
background to explain things and make it relevant;
again slides may be disproportionately useful in
such circumstances.

Duration

As usual the content affects the duration. Logistics may too. For example, if you are addressing staff who do not report to you, their manager may be prepared to spare them for only so long – thus being reasonable about time may help secure other sessions in the longer term.

Speaker's notes

The members of the audience are in effect your customers, so think about what you need to achieve through the session and make sure you have adequate notes in front of you to enable you to do so in a way that satisfies them.

Useful quotes

'There is only one boss: the customer. And he can fire everybody in the company, from the chairman down, simply by spending his money somewhere else.'
Sam Walton

'The consumer is not a moron, she's your wife.'
David Ogilvy

'WARNING: customers are perishable.'
Sign in department store

Speaking to customers

In many ways there is no more important group. Customers are fundamental to any organisation's success. They may need speaking to in person on many occasions, some where you visit them, some where they visit you and some at other events (a trade fair or conference, perhaps). Always this needs doing with care, always it is a significant opportunity.

Always too it is worth bearing in mind that whatever is said and however it is put over, it personalises an image already built up of the organisation and the way it works, and obtained from the wealth of less personal communications of which they are in receipt. These include everything from advertising to letters from your accounts department chasing for payment of your invoices.

Maximising the opportunity

The ultimate opportunity is to play a part in making them buy. This may be for the first time or to encourage ongoing business.

En route to that a number of things may be necessary, these include.

◆ Informing them (about everything from news of new products to promotional activity or financial terms.

◆ Persuading them – often anything addressed to customers is in the nature of selling.

◆ Differentiating yourselves from competition (after all, however good your product or service, others no doubt make strong claims also).

These three need thinking about and skilfully blending together.

Additionally, you may well want to thank them for past business (though do not become like Uriah Heep), flatter them (carefully) or involve them, for instance canvassing their opinions or creating and building business partnerships.

Key things to include

Clear information pitched in terms that are persuasive (for example, stressing the benefits – this takes us beyond our brief into the whole area of sales skills).

A focus on something specific; as opportunities to address customers may be limited (certainly in terms of what you would like). There is a danger of throwing everything in and not doing justice to it all.

Views presented from their point of view.

Some genuine news and excitement.

Dangers to avoid

Never – ever – ask for customers *to support you*. This can all too easily sound as if it is no more than asking them to do you a favour (why should they?). You have to earn their support. In any case, you may be better to talk in terms such as suggesting *You take advantage of this opportunity*.

An approach that mentions everything in sight (see above).

An introspective approach with everything starting *I, we* or *the company* when what is looked for is something that reflects their point of view, their needs and perspective.

Creating a clear structure

The clarity with which things are done, evidence of care and preparation and a sound, logical structure are all especially important here as customers will infer a lack of respect for them if such things are not in evidence.

Beginning

◆ If customer gatherings are rare then there is a need to make it feel a bit special.

◆ Start with an immediate positive feel expressing something about the benefit of the occasion for those attending.

◆ Set out a well considered and well organised agenda.

◆ If customers are visiting you, make them feel at home and spell out how administrative matters will be dealt with (what happens if there are messages for them, for instance).

Middle
◆ Follow the agenda.

◆ Maintain interest (and excitement?) throughout.

◆ Keep your eye on the objectives (to sell), but in parallel with their viewpoint.

◆ Allow as much participation as is appropriate.

End
◆ You want people to remember – and act on – this session, so make the action clear (and easy) and always finish on a high note.

NOTE: Have any follow up action ready and spell out what it will be. For example, having a letter on their desks the following morning may take a little organising, but it can be impressive and thus worthwhile.

Overall
◆ Any session must have clear objectives and, while this is always important, it is especially so that they are couched in terms of the audience – the customers.

◆ In terms of manner, always welcoming, appreciative and enthusiastic – without going over the top in any of these ways. Essentially it is useful to see this as a session that always focuses outward.

Additional dimensions
◆ Usually there will be a specific focus here, like the launch of one specific new product, but other elements need positioning carefully. There should not be too many of them and they should not be allowed to act to obscure the main purpose.

Visual aids
◆ Anything that is used should not just be clear, but high quality (as it reflects your perceived professionalism).

◆ If you are speaking to a group of people from one customer it looks good to have their logo on your slides.

Duration

Whatever the duration it is important to publish it – and then to stick to time.

You may also want to allow for hospitality, the informal chat in any break may be very useful to all present.

Never try to do more than you can do justice too, it will always end up looking like a failure of organisation or planning and thus as a lack of courtesy or respect to those attending.

Speaker's notes

Certainly sufficient for you not to lose your way on what is an important occasion. Ensure a clear link between your notes and any visuals and handouts.

Useful quotes

'The customer is always right.' *H. Gordon Selfridge*

'Satisfying the customer is a race without finish.'
Vernon Maxmin

'For every customer who complains, fifty walk.'
Anon

Instigating a change

Two key points are worth bearing in mind:

◆ Everyone is in favour of change. Change is a good thing – right up to the moment when someone comes into your office and says *Right, there are going to be some changes **here!*** What happens in these circumstances? Many people are suspicious and fear the worst. Whether the objective is positive (improving performance) or negative (reducing costs), the natural reaction seems to be to anticipate difficulties. So, if this is the case (and it is), the only response is to address the issue and get past this reaction to make change possible. As Louise L. Hay said *Change is usually what we want the other person to do.*

◆ Change is the norm. We live in a dynamic world. Any organisation must respond to changes of all sorts: these may include competitive action, technical development, government legislation, environmental controls, financial restriction and more. They may be prompted internally or externally; or both. Change is not an option, something to do if it fits in, it is essential to corporate survival.

Maximising the opportunity

To ensure that:

- ◆ The need for change, and the potential results of it, are accepted (together perhaps with the dangers of *not* changing.

- ◆ Any downsides are explained and minimised (and balanced against the advantages).

- ◆ Action is spelt out and co-operation is agreed.

In addition, to ensure that the action to make the change goes ahead to plan and on time. Beyond that, the opportunity is in the nature of the change whether this is in money made or saved, improved customer service and subsequent sales, increased productivity of some sort or anything else.

Key things to include

Provide adequate background and explanation. Never just say *This is going to change*, explain why and how and what the results will be, including those for the individuals.

Have a good overall structure, deal systematically with the detail and make clear how you will do so.

Make a link with something similar to the topic/project under discussion. Using this as an example helps people's imagination. If you pick carefully and conjure up memories of how much easier something else was than anticipated, how well it worked and how little it disrupted other things this will help remove fears.

Mention specifically: who will do what, the timing and any new targets.

Dangers to avoid

Muddling the past and the future will create confusion. Deal separately with what has happened in the past, and now, and what the situation will be for the future.

Allowing people to make unwarranted assumptions about any negative aspects, by not addressing this aspect up front.

While the dangers of taking no action may be considerable, and may need highlighting and exemplifying, do not allow this to predominate so that the session becomes primarily doom and gloom in nature.

Creating a clear structure

Beginning

◆ You need a clear statement of purpose, coupled with something early on that addresses people's natural fears (especially personal rather than corporate ones).

Middle

◆ Be sure that your 'agenda' addresses the various different intentions you may well have separately.

◆ Be sure you keep a cohesive flow and that the overall effect does not become ragged.

End

◆ Given the complexity inherent here, a summary is likely to be important. Recap the reasons and what is to be gained and give emphasis to the action, timing etc that will make implementation possible.

Overall

◆ The intention here should be to combine allaying fears with a positive approach to whatever needs to be done and a clear guide to action. The details of whatever is being discussed need to be clear, together with the reasons for change. Remember people dislike tinkering and they dislike just being told – *do this because I say so.* Without explanation and background it will always be more difficult to get the need for change accepted

◆ In terms of manner, your confidence in dealing with the matter should show. Other feelings may be there (surprise or concern perhaps), but people should take on board your confidence in a considered response.

Additional dimensions

Given the fact that 'change is the norm', one thing that every individual session of this sort should address is that fact. The need for change needs to be regularly described as normal, positive and necessary. Every session can play a part in making the next one go better because there is a greater acceptance of the facts.

Visual aids

The detail involved in such a session makes the use of visual aids desirable. These can be used to control the session and ensure a good structure is followed, and to assist explanation and spell out action required.

Duration

◆ As long as the topic demands, but be sure not to underestimate the time needed for the early stages (background and explanation).

Speaker's notes

Whatever allows you to proceed purposefully and do the job necessary.

Useful quotes

'If it ain't broke, break it.'   *Richard Pascale*

'Every organisation has to prepare for the abandonment of everything it does.'*Peter Drucker*

'Change is only another word for growth, another synonym for learning. We can all do it if we want.'
                            Charles Handy

'When you're through changing, you're through. Change is a process, not a goal; a journey, not a destination.'   *Robert Kriegal and David Brandt*

Welcoming a newcomer (or visitor)

I know one company where it is a joke that anyone joining the organisation spends several weeks with everyone else assuming that they are there to mend the photocopier because no introductions are ever made.

While you cannot gather the whole organisation together every time a new member of staff joins, it may be possible in a smaller organisation, certainly in a department, and does have some positive benefits. Occasions when outsider visits may well be important (one category of people here may be customers), are reviewed as a separate topic.

Maximising the opportunity

There are three distinct opportunities here:

- ◆ The first is both a courtesy to the newcomer or visitor and, of course, an opportunity for them to meet others (speeding up communications that will follow).

- ◆ The second is to put over information to them about the organisation, recent or planned developments or whatever is relevant.

- ◆ The third is that it creates a session at which everyone is present and that can be utilised for more general or separate purposes. This is especially useful if there is something timely to mention or if people have not, in fact, got together for a while.

It may be the kind of session that is sometimes conducted in a social fashion – with a welcome drink, for instance.

Key things to include

The first thing is to express a genuine welcome to the individual and make any specific individual introductions that are necessary. This can often be a two way process: you need to describe the visitor or newcomer to the group and vice versa.

Beyond that you need to think about two things. First, making a brief description work hard. Whether you are describing the organisation, a department or touching on some topical development, you have to encapsulate the key elements involved succinctly. This links to preparation as more care is often necessary if you are to keep something brief and yet make it useful.

Secondly, you need to think through what to talk about, what to omit and then prioritise. In other words you must be clear what gets a mention, what gets a summary and what is just a hint. This selection process is an important part of making anything of this nature work without overextending it.

Dangers to avoid

The main danger is that courtesy to the newcomer or visitor is allowed to get lost as the opportunity to mention other matters crowds it out.

It is worth noting that it could be that the person is *not* welcome. For example, if someone much liked has left (worse if it is unavoidable as with say ill health), or if a visitor is a consultant or someone from head office present to take unpleasant action (cut costs or people) then you will not instinctively welcome them with open arms. There is, however, a job to be done. If people need to work with them then the scene must be set positively; more so when any difficulty is not of their making (indeed they may be unaware of it). If this kind of situation is not addressed then an opportunity will be missed and harm may result.

Failure to prepare – especially in terms of prioritising content – can lead to a rambling approach and overextend the time inappropriately.

Ccreating a clear structure

Beginning

◆ Ensure a suitable immediate focus on the 'guest' at the start.

◆ Make it clear what you will do – to introduce them, to speak to them about their visit/arrival and to make use of the opportunity to speak to all.

Middle

◆ This is probably a short, sharp session but it still needs to be kept well organised.

◆ Always end the main points with a firm link back to the individual.

End

◆ Address final remarks to the newcomer/visitor and end, with sincerity, on a high note.

Overall

◆ This should be straightforward. But it needs to be done in a way that makes it clear that it is not simply 'going through the motions', and may need to link to topical matters. For example, maybe you have had three newcomers in the last month and you do not want it to sound as if a mass exodus is under way; maybe a long awaited strengthening of the team is significant just ahead of a busy patch or challenging project. For a visitor there may well be an emphasis on something topical and positive or interesting.

◆ In terms of manner, you need to make this sound genuine and positive, and if it is real break from the routine; this can be in evidence also.

Additional dimensions

◆ A little humour here may well be appropriate.

◆ It may also be useful to flag things that you touch on necessarily briefly as areas that will be explained more fully later – *You will get a chance to spend more time with Barry and he will give you chapter and verse about what his team get up to.*

◆ Always bear in mind with a visitor (even from elsewhere in the organisation) the things you do *not* want to expose to an outsider.

◆ Consider if appropriate other aspects of welcome, a round of applause for instance, and how you organise it.

◆ Consider also where a visitor comes from. Their being from a customer, from out of town or from overseas may warrant special mention (and a different degree of detail being given).

Visual aids
◆ The likelihood is nothing like slides will be appropriate or used.

◆ The one exception is people – you may want to point people out to the newcomer, get them to stand up for a moment or even to introduce themselves (in which case do they need some notice of what to do?).

Duration
This is unlikely to be a long session, particularly as it should not be so overextended as to major on peripheral

issues; more so if it is in a social setting as it would be over drinks.

Speaker's notes

The less formal the session the less you will need. A few cards, which can be dealt with easily as you stand within a group, may be all that is necessary.

Useful quotes

'Make three correct guesses consecutively and you will establish a reputation as an expert.'

Laurence J. Peter

'Recruitment is easy. Find and appoint a good candidate. Watch and see if they perform satisfactorily. If their performance proves unsatisfactory – don't appoint them.'   *Overheard*

'The man who makes no mistakes does not make anything.'   *Edward John Phelps*

Introducing yourself

If you are seeking a new job, then success may come sooner if you do not regard your c.v. as a standard document. It needs tailoring depending on the kind of job and organisation towards which you are directing your applications. So too with introductions; you must not have a kind of 'stock' few introductory remarks – you need to think about what it is best to say in every different circumstance.

This is true if you are new to an organisation and introducing yourself for the first time to a group of new colleagues. It is true also if you simply have to introduce yourself to new people in any situation (this might include a group of customers or the audience at a conference – perhaps a trade or industry event – which you have been persuaded to address).

Maximising the opportunity

Like a number of the topics in this book, this one may offer the option of your having multiple intentions. If so you need to be clear in your own mind what they are and what your priorities should be. Certainly you can aim to:

◆ Inform people (about everything from your background and your experience to your skills and attitudes).

◆ Influence the way you are perceived, and this may

mean emphasising particular characteristics. You may want to be seen as professional, confident, expert, knowledgeable, well organised, caring, experienced, reliable, objective, approachable, trustworthy, an achiever – and more. You may also want to minimise other factors, for example to overcome the thought that your young age precludes your having sufficient experience or competence to do something.

♦ Affect the way in which people relate to you; for example, to make consultation or co-operation more likely and thus make action and implementation easier to achieve.

Key things to include

The two key things are background and achievements, but there are many things to be considered in matching a particular introduction to its purpose:

♦ Jobs held and previous employers.

♦ Projects handled (or in which you have been involved) and their success.

♦ Achievements beyond job results (such things as receiving an award – or writing a book!).

♦ International involvement.

♦ Publicity moments (say speaking at an event or being interviewed on radio).

- Anecdotes about past work life, people and incidents.

- Likes and dislikes.

- Manner and style (*Whatever else, I am a manager who is always prepared to listen*).

- Peripheral activities (being on an external committee or doing work with a trade or professional body).

You may also have to link whatever you choose to say to a description of your role 'on the day' – *Today I am in the Chair...I am here as a spokesman for...* even if you need to add *For my sins, I...* Additionally, always match what you choose to say to the circumstances of the event and the audience.

There is one more aspect here that is worth a digression: that of introducing your company – see box.

Talking about your organisation

At public training events one ubiquitous ritual is the early moment when participants introduce themselves. As a trainer conducting this kind of event I have heard a great many of them over the years. If there is one thing that people might be expected to talk about with some fluency this is surely it. Often this is not so, and a few garbled

---

sentences fail to describe it very well and totally fail to do it justice.

Like anything that is highly selective this does present some problems. A complete history and description of what the organisation does, its organisational structure and so on would take hours. So you need to think about what to say (and what not to say) as well as how to put it. Bear your audience in mind and consider what sort of detail they will find useful and interesting. People from outside on some sort of technical visit will want the focus on the technical side. Others need a different emphasis.

Describe everything clearly (if you do not do so people are entitled to doubt everything else you say). Make it interesting and make it live (for example, it may be more meaningful to say your organisation *is twice the size of How-to-Books*, than simply to quote its precise turnover). Concentrate on positive things: successes, new ventures, etc and people issues (and you can include customers in this).

Do not let familiarity with what you are talking about lead to your not thinking about it, or abbreviating it out of sheer boredom.

A considered, clear and descriptive résumé positively and enthusiastically delivered can start sessions

> where it needs to be done well. Better still if you can think of something novel or memorable. I remember hearing a senior manager of the part of ICI that makes, among other things, shotgun cartridges speak at a marketing conference attended mainly by people from FMCG companies (Fast Moving Consumer Goods). He described himself as marketing *the fastest moving product represented by those attending!*

Dangers to avoid

The chief one is an 'I, I, I' approach. It can sound like an introspective list *I am . . . I have done . . . I do . . .* and thus become unappealing.

Another is to include too much, particularly unnecessary detail or matters from too far back.

Modesty can be dangerous too: whether used too little or too much.

Creating a clear structure

Beginning
- ◆ It may often be appropriate to make it clear why people need you to say anything. Doing so may be no more than a courtesy, or it may be very specific. For example, I conduct workshops on making presentations at the start of which it is useful for

participants to have some knowledge of what I have done in this respect (to make clear I speak about it largely from experience).

Middle

◆ Rather than simply listing *I did this...* find other ways of putting things. I am often asked to give some background to my consulting and training work. Rather than always say what I have done and start with the 'I', I might start with the client *When Company X wanted to beef up their product launch in Singapore, I found myself making presentations on their behalf to...* Alternatively, you can start with results *The proportion of written proposals producing business has increased since I conducted a proposal writing course for...*

End

Perhaps a touch of modesty provides a link to what follows *Enough of this, let's turn now to...*

Overall

◆ The most important thing here is not an information point – what you tell people about yourself. It is about the impression you give and thus how people think about you, and perhaps then relate to you afterwards.

◆ In terms of manner, you need to think carefully. You cannot pretend to be something you are not (at least not for long), but you may usefully emphasise those characteristics that you *want* people to appreciate are there. You need to consider what these characteristics are and how you put them across.

Additional dimensions

◆ Bear in mind that introducing yourself may not be all that is required. If your introduction is linked to something else you will then do, then the two must sit comfortably together and the introduction must usually be positioned so as not to overpower the remainder of your session, though the introduction is likely to come first.

Visual aids

◆ In many circumstances nothing will be needed or appropriate here.

◆ Be careful if you are tempted to use a slide as a kind of title page to a talk that must simply start with a brief introduction about yourself. These may serve a useful purpose, being part of spelling out an agenda or making clear the spelling of your name, or your position in the organisation. More often they have no real role. They are included only out of habit and an 'automatic pilot' approach to preparation, and they succeed only in looking pretentious.

Duration

Keep it brief. It is very easy for what you do to turn into an indulgence or something inappropriately promotional. Make what you do say work hard by all means and have clear objectives in mind, but keep it short.

Speaker's notes

Use as necessary, but do not appear to have to consult them to remind you what your name is or where you went to university!

Useful quotes

'Experience isn't interesting until it begins to repeat itself – in fact, till it does that, it hardly is experience.'

Elizabeth Bowen

'A moment's insight is sometimes worth a life's experience.' *Oliver Wendell Holmes*

'Specialist – A man who knows more and more about less and less.' *William James Mayo*

Scotching rumours

This should be something that is necessary only rarely. When it is, however, there is some urgency about correcting the situation and acting to prevent damage or to correct – or reverse – any damage that has already been done. Rumours arise for all sorts of reasons. They may be created through misunderstandings, silence and wrong assumption, or they may be started with malicious intent. They may become more extreme fuelled by people's worry or fear, and they can seemingly spread with the speed of light.

Maximising the opportunity

There are a number of things that you might want to do. The first is surely to clarify and set the record straight. Beyond that you may want to get the message across that:

◆ Rumours are damaging and the temptation to listen to them and spread them should be resisted.

◆ People should ask about anything which they are unclear about or fear about which they are getting inaccurate information about.

◆ The intentional intent of individuals to misinform other people, or worse to stir up unrest, will not be tolerated.

In addition, you may want to address and explain reasons why rumours have occurred (maybe silence by management on some key issue inevitably gave rise to speculation – if so then an apology may be due as well as an explanation).

Key things to include

The content here is likely to be straightforward:

◆ A sensible and succinct recap (after all not everyone may have heard the rumour or heard it in the same form).

◆ A clear explanation of the true situation.

◆ Or: a clear statement that no information can be forthcoming for the moment, a clear explanation as to *why* this is so and a specific promise to come back to people at a stated time.

◆ Perhaps some reprimand regarding the rumour-mongering (though a public occasion may not be the place to direct remarks at individuals).

Dangers to avoid

The key thing is not to make matters worse. If you give even a hint of cover-up, and no real explanations, then you will compound people's fear of the worst. If you seem to be reacting in panic, then again people may assume the worst, especially if they find what you have to say unconvincing.

Another danger is a perceived smokescreen. Your explanation is there, but is lost amongst all sorts of blandishments and the lack of a clear message is again taken negatively.

Creating a clear structure

Beginning

◆ Be very clear up front about what you are going to do. If there is something that must remain confidential (and if so there had better ultimately be a good reason for it) say so early on, do not let people think an answer is going to be forthcoming and then disappoint them.

◆ If clear explanation is in any sense lengthy then set out a clear agenda.

◆ Address any fears early on (for example, if rumour has it there are to be redundancies and there are not, say so at once, though your agenda may include setting out other changes that *are* set to occur).

Middle

◆ Remain organised and clear throughout.

◆ Consider when to allow questions (doing so early as you proceed may help act to quell fears *There can't be anything to worry about if they're doing that).*

◆ Be careful about any humour you use. If people have been seriously worried, or confused, in some way, your making light of it may be taken the wrong way.

◆ Separate the incorrect from the correct, saying what *will* happen or be the case and what will *not*.

End

◆ Do not rush to a conclusion.

◆ Ensure there are no loose ends left and that people have no further questions.

◆ If follow-up communications are necessary say so and give a clear timetable for what will happen (*I will let you have more information by the end of the month*); and then *always* report back as promised.

Overall

◆ Clarity must prevail and be obvious throughout.

◆ In terms of manner, you need to consider the tone that you adopt (how serious), and speak with authority and precision in a way that gives real confidence. There may even need to be a feeling of something heavier (a threat?) making it clear that rumour-mongering stops right here and now.

Additional dimensions

◆ Most of the additional matters here are likely to be for other occasions (for example, action to inhibit the spreading of further rumours or the setting out of real new plans at an appropriate time).

◆ It might be appropriate at once, however, to comment on policy, stating for instance how you intend to be as open as possible about things and setting out what that means.

Visual aids

◆ Force of personality and tone should predominate here. If rumours are about something inherently difficult to explain (figures, perhaps) then slides may help.

Duration

Get to the point and do not prolong such a session, drawing it out or going round the houses may be read as evasion or uncertainty. Otherwise it needs as long as it takes to resolve matters and ensure clarity and truth again hold sway.

Speaker's notes

These will reflect the subject of the rumours, the complexity of the response and the duration of what is said. Given the importance of accuracy, they must be designed to ensure exactly that.

Useful quotes

'Things are going to get worse before they get worse.'
                                                    Lilly Tomlin

'It takes two to speak the truth – one to speak and another to hear.'   *Henry David Thoreau*

'Speech was given to man to disguise his thoughts.'
                                                    Talleyrand

---

Sounding a warning

The comments that follow under this heading are perhaps best described as saying '*No*' or '*This will not happen*'. What you are saying no to may range widely, and the situation may be long or short – no this week or no forever (though *forever* is a very long time, and perhaps nothing is ruled out literally forever).

The situation here can sound a warning but hold the action. Indeed it may aim to do more, to put something on one side so that it ceases to distract and take up time. Even postponing something temporarily may be useful. If growth indicates you will have to move offices, with all the attendant upheaval that suggests, then saying *Yes, we will have to move* and setting out some parameters about how the disruption will be mitigated is one thing. This is a warning sounded well ahead. Saying *But we will definitely not be moving for eighteen months* can act to postpone the process which will lock in nearer the time. This is in effect a warning not to let the impending move interfere with current operations.

Maximising the opportunity

Obviously the first, and perhaps the most important, thing here is to prevent something occurring. Depending on the circumstances, you may well want to:

◆ Explain external dangers and how they will affect people – *The recession will limit our ability to expand as ideally as we would wish, requests for additional funds for X are ruled out at least for the next six months.*

◆ Similarly with internal dangers – *The merger is going to mean a good bit of reorganising, but we cannot let this hold up our X project – so let's hear no suggestions that it should, please.*

◆ Clarify or lay down rules – *In future expense claims must be in on time, no claim, no money and repayment will have to wait until the following month.*

Key things to include

The key things are to:

◆ Give any necessary background.

◆ Spell out the danger.

◆ Deal with any balancing factors.

◆ Set out the rules and link to policy.

Deal carefully with personal issues. The warning may be directed firmly to stop staff doing something – *No one is to use the Reception area – where there are nearly always customers waiting – as a meeting place, especially not to chat and exchange gossip.* It may be useful to single out examples in such circumstances, equally it can do more harm than good; so care is necessary.

Dangers to avoid

The greatest danger is that what you say comes over without conviction or without power. You need to be able to say *No* in a way that makes it one hundred percent clear that you do not mean *Maybe*. People have to believe that you mean what you say. This is especially true if there is an *Or else* element to the message; if you make threats you must normally be prepared to see them through or see your authority devalued for the future.

Similarly if you label something *Final warning* it had better be just that. Getting a reputation for crying wolf is not to recommended.

Clear structure

Beginning

◆ The more serious the matter the greater the need to get straight to the point.

◆ Then spell out the agenda and, if both are involved, split the positive and the negative elements of what you have to say.

Middle

◆ Use a logical approach and do not digress if you want to people to remain fixed on the main message.

End

◆ This may need a stern tone and a heavy sentiment to end with. Certainly the ending must aim to restate the importance of what has been said – and make it stick.

Overall

◆ In terms of manner, the tone is the most important thing here. No sign of panic must be in evidence and a calm, considered and positive approach must predominate. Control any anger that you might feel. There is a place occasionally for a display of anger, but never for a loss of temper.

◆ If you are saying *Do not do this* or *Watch out for that* then maybe there are things to say that can add a positive note.

Additional dimensions

◆ As the overall topic here may be negative it may be worth seeing if you can link a warning to other, less negative matters, though sometimes the importance necessitates a stark, isolated statement to produce the impact that you want.

Visual aids

◆ A short, sharp shock warning probably needs nothing but your own weight behind it, but a complex issue needs clear explanation. So if getting people to take heed of the warning is vital you will want to do justice to the explanation and visuals may help.

Duration

The topic of the session will dictate this. Firmness will be enhanced by your being succinct in what you say, so it may be wise not to go on too long (though you need to give sufficient time to background and explaining the why of the matter).

Speaker's notes

Anything you have in front of you must be clear and, where you want to sound firm, you may want to think about the precise words you use and how you can give it suitable weight.

Useful quotes

'The future has a way of arriving unannounced.'

George F. Will

'The best way to win an argument is to begin by being right.'   *Jill Ruckelshaus*

'It's a rare person who wants to hear what he doesn't want to hear.'   *Dick Cavett*

'Obstacles are made to be overcome.'   *Proverb*

Launching something new

Much as I love bookshops (display this one prominently, please), one thing about them regularly annoys me. It is their definition of the word *New*. Take, for example the film of *The Lord of the Rings,* a recent blockbuster movie. Bookshops, understandably, display the book on some scale. But many have it labelled *New*. It may be many things, but new it is not.

You should not devalue the concept. If something is genuinely new then this makes it more interesting and is a way of getting people to take notice, but save such announcements for real 'news'.

Maximising the opportunity

The opportunity is to draw attention to something, and often to prompt action, and to do so by using the newness to enhance the process. It might be something dramatic like a company launching a new product; something that will affect many people around the organisation and which may demand an immediate added dimension for those with a customer care role. Alternatively, it might be something more mundane – like the adoption of a new system – though there too the implications might well be important.

Key things to include

The first thing is to describe the news in clear and enthusiastic terms.

You may also want to link past and future – *this is how it was, but now...!*

You might just want to add provisos, for example if you are telling people at an early stage they may be required to keep it quiet and not pass it on further for the moment (if so explain why).

Beyond this the content will link to whatever the news is and, more particularly, to what the implications of it may be. Does action follow? If so what is that action?

Dangers to avoid

If something is inherently interesting do not let that overpower the specific interest you want people to take in it. To take the example of a new product again, this might stand considerable investigation as staff inspect it, try it or taste it. But if the action is to talk about it, take orders for it – whatever – then there must be a focus on that aspect. On the other hand do not switch off enthusiasm for something, it can be harnessed to link to the action people must take.

Creating a clear structure

Beginning

◆ This is something that can be started with some

excitement. This might be simply saying *Good news!* Or it might be that the new thing itself, in suitably encapsulated form is the first thing said.

Middle

◆ Here the structure will be dictated primarily by the nature of what it is that is new. Something complex may need spelling out. Or it may be the implications that need to be organised: immediate impact and what follows later, for instance.

◆ It is possible, of course, that something new may have difficult or negative connotations in which case the handling of it may need to be done differently.

End

◆ Probably, certainly for something new and good, this needs a punchy ending, something that refers back to the fact of what is new, for example to invite comments (as might be done with a new product – *Have a proper look, try it, and let me know what you think*).

Overall:

◆ In terms of manner, enthusiasm is important (assuming that new is, in one way or another, good), also a feeling of certainty – *this will be . . .* (not *I think . . .* and rarely *I hope . . .*).

Additional dimensions

◆ The key thing here is implications. Sometimes an announcement of something new is enough, indeed it might be the end of a long wait during which many details have been announced and discussed. On other occasions the announcement itself may be brief but immediately necessitates spelling out an action plan.

Visual aids

◆ Are you talking about something you can show? If it is new then, by definition, people will be unfamiliar with it, so show it if at all possible. Whether it is a form they must complete, or an advertisement that your customers will soon see, it is difficult to describe, but easy to demonstrate.

Duration

As has been said, this may range wide from a simple announcement to something much longer if there are other issues to be addressed. With interesting new developments that will affect people, or that need their active support, take time to do the matter justice or what should be a positive occasion can seen unreasonably curtailed and will fail to do the intentions justice.

Speaker's notes

Like the duration, what is necessary here may vary a good deal and is prescribed by the overall nature of what is to be done.

Useful quotes

'If we do not find anything pleasant, at least we shall find something new.'   *Voltaire*

'Innovation has a lot to do with your ability to recognise surprising and unusual phenomena.'
Herbert Simon

'News: anything that makes a woman say "For heaven's sake." '   *Edgar Watson Howe*

'If they haven't heard it before, it's original.'
Gene Fowler

Marking an anniversary

What might this be? It might relate to a person: spending so long with the organisation, or in a particular job. It might relate to the organisation: formed fifty years ago. Or to some element of the overall organisation: a landmark for a product, process or location.

In a sense this is contrived news, only of significance because the human mind likes neatness and responds to a round number. But it may imply more than this; a person sticking at something with commendable persistence, perhaps. If you use such events to link to people's motivation, or externally to garner publicity, then you will want to pick sensible ones that have some real substance or meaning. So five years with the organisation might warrant a mention, but not much more, whereas ten years is a real occasion, maybe one that suggests a celebration of some sort – and at which something needs to be said.

Maximising the opportunity

There are two separate areas of opportunity here. One is individual – motivating someone through congratulations about their achievement. The other is about the organisation (or something it has done) and needs linking to the individuals. For example, the anniversary of the setting up of an organisation is a milestone for the founder, they were there, and maybe personal congratulations are in order.

For others, perhaps more recently with the organisation, the link is one by proxy, there is a reflected glory as it were in being there in, say, the fiftieth year.

Whatever the situation there is an easy link that can be made with the future; and thus with action – *Fifty successful years! We want to be sure it continues, an immediate task that will help is to . . .*

Key things to include
Credit where credit is due as appropriate for the occasion.

There should be a clear distinction between matters of the past and the future.

A link between one person's success and encouragement to others (especially internally).

A link between the current occasion and specific future plans.

Dangers to avoid
Exaggerating the importance of something, or rather failing to make it sound important and thus making its mention or celebration seem contrived or simply inappropriate.

Being flippant or sounding insincere about something, especially when you then use its importance as a call for action.

Creating a clear structure

Beginning

◆ Start with a clear focus on the occasion, and if appropriate the person.

◆ Make any appropriate congratulations clear – and sincere.

Middle

◆ The key thing is either to keep it simple or to use a structure that separates what you say about the occasion neatly from what you use it as a rationale to say beyond that, and do so in a way that does not allow the original intention to be sidelined.

End

◆ The best structure probably ends up where it began, with the present occasion.

◆ Probably any individual presentation (from flowers to a gift) is best done at the end and used as a finish – though you could consider placing this elsewhere in a speech that digresses extensively on to other matters.

Overall

◆ In terms of manner, the overall tone is most likely to need to be upbeat and this should be maintained. You are unlikely to celebrate the anniversary of a disaster, but resist linking an event (say) ten years back to something like a current struggle to achieve

growth in a recession or resist a hostile take-over.
So, a positive note throughout will probably work
best.

Additional dimensions
◆ This is something about which you might speak to
   outsiders (for example, press or customers). If so the
   extra importance of this needs to be reflected. Most
   importantly you must have something tangible to
   say, and usually this means something that goes
   beyond just the announcement and most often
   something that looks ahead.

Visual aids
◆ Only useful for the more formal occasion and
   where the mention of the anniversary takes you
   beyond the occasion and there is more to talk
   about.

◆ More likely to be necessary for external
   presentations.

Duration

Like many topics the duration is decided by the kind of
occasion (a word at a celebration party is different from
a word at a planning meeting). Unless the occasion is of
clear and major import, do not let the duration extend
inappropriately. Keep it tight.

Speaker's notes

What is necessary here will need to relate to the nature of the occasion and how it is being used. If it is an opportunity for a call to action, then the details of this need to be clear in front of you.

Useful quotes

'Nothing great was achieved without enthusiasm.'
Ralph Waldo Emerson

'It is as hard to stay on top as it is to get there.'
Hugh Cudlipp

'One never notices what has been done; one can only see what remains to be done.'   *Marie Curie*

'To achieve great things we must live as if we are never going to die.'   *Marquis de Vauvenargues*

Highlighting a key issue

Here such a session is taken as addressing something you want to bring to the front of people's minds, either temporarily or permanently (in the latter case what you say on one occasion may be part of an ongoing campaign to create and maintain awareness). Such issues might include overall factors such as productivity or accuracy, as well as more specific things like good timekeeping or the need for prompt telephone answering in a department involved with customer care.

Maximising the opportunity

The opportunity is not to highlight something for the sake of it, or to highlight it in such a way that action follows, and often so that it is maintained consistently thereafter. To take a simple example, if you highlight the need for good timekeeping then you do not just want people to turn up on time tomorrow, you want them to be on time every day.

Key things to include

Some decisions are needed here about what to include and what not to include. For example, if highlighting something is designed to improve it, do you want to castigate past performance in some way or is it going to be better just to enthuse people to do better? Anyway it may be that past performance *was* good, but new circumstances demand something different again; after all many managers subscribe to the view that *even the best performance can be improved.*

That said, you need to mix and match the following:

◆ A past situation – that must not continue or which can be built on.

◆ The reasons for change – if change is implied.

◆ The benefits of concentrating unrelentingly on whatever is being highlighted; demonstrating clearly why it is worth the effort.

◆ The penalty or dangers of not so doing.

◆ Any incentive, personal or corporate, for getting it right.

Given the list above, deciding the structure and sequence that you will employ is also important.

Dangers to avoid

Avoid being seen to nag or 'cry wolf'. If your tone and approach, or the frequency of your inducements, are seen as exaggerated or over the top, then what they say will be devalued, perhaps ignored. Care may be necessary not to use inflammatory language – do you mean *unacceptable* or is something a little softer more appropriate?

Creating a clear structure

Beginning

◆ Whether what you do is the first highlighting or yet another reminder, make it clear what you are doing. If is a 'yet again' speech say so, and find a way to make what you have to say fresh early on.

◆ Spell out your agenda. Is this to be just a word of reminder or do you need to review real detail?

Middle

◆ Fit the main content to the substance of what needs to be done: a lengthy session will need more structure, a shorter one will need more precision, careful choice of words and some real clout to make its message stick.

End

◆ Whatever the nature of the session it is likely to need a punchy finish, one that is action orientated.

Overall

◆ The overall intention, beyond explaining, should be to kick-start action and play its part if necessary in changing or reinforcing attitudes.

◆ To do this it is important that people accept the message (agreeing that it is necessary and the results are worthwhile), make it attractive (so that people *want* to do their best) and manageable (so that people feel it is not the last straw and that they can accommodate the action necessary without jeopardising other responsibilities).

◆ In terms of manner, a degree of enthusiasm is necessary (to help show people that you really do believe this is important), together with a feeling that the main content is well considered.

Additional dimensions

◆ Think about how you can put things in terms of the individuals you are addressing. You may think automatically in terms of financial years for example, but younger staff may think Friday week is long term. One example here is amortising figures; the overall corporate figures may just seem like enormous, unimaginable numbers whereas what is necessary per week or per month may make more sense.

◆ Think too of how to put over any necessary empathy. If you want people to respond more quickly – *think speed* – then get them to put themselves in the shoes of those that more rapid response will help in order to bring the situation to life.

Visual aids

◆ An ongoing campaign of focusing on key issues

might benefit from a slogan and that might lend itself to visual aids or the enhancement of them. One organisation adopting a focus on achieving key priorities usefully employed the slogan *Getting rid of the alligators* (based on the old maxim about objectives that *It is difficult to remember that the objective was to drain the swamp when you are up to your arse in alligators*).

Duration

The duration here can vary owing to the range of different types of session that might come under this heading. The key specific thing to bear in mind here is that undue length might be construed as being unduly heavy or simply inappropriate – *Yea, yea – we know that*. If this happens the effectiveness of the message may be diluted. As ever therefore, chosen duration should be a considered decision not just something 'that happens'.

Speaker's notes

Like duration above what is appropriate here will vary depending on the nature of the session. Repeated pleas should not use the same old platitudes, so do not recycle your old notes – and phrases. Revisit your objectives and prepare accordingly, then have your updated notes in front of you.

Useful quotes

'The only sure thing is that in business there are no sure things.'

Akio Morita

'A diplomat is a person who can tell you to go to hell in such a way that you look forward to the trip.'

Caskie Stinnett

'Perseverance capitalises inspiration.' *Alex F. Osborn*

'You have to be efficient if you're going to be lazy.'

Shirley Conran

Spelling out plans

One of the management buzzwords of recent years was 'empowerment', a word that encapsulated the thought of creating a commitment to things with staff which, matched by giving them responsibility, allowed them to carry matters through with little or no supervision. Put this together with another slightly jargon phrase, that of the concept of 'ownership', people committing more easily to a plan that is 'theirs' and together these set the scene for what needs to be done here.

Involvement is one thing: people like it if consultation leads up to plans being implemented. This is somewhat beyond our brief here, suffice it to say that this is a good thing and makes effective implementation more likely. Understanding is another – people will always be more able and willing to carry through something that is explained, and which they therefore understand (well, provided the explanation is clear!), that if they are just told *do this*.

Maximising the opportunity

The opportunity is clear:

◆ To inform people what a plan is.

◆ To convince them it is sensible and should be supported.

◆ To lay out the action elements, what needs to be done, by whom and when.

♦ To make it appear manageable.

♦ To motivate so that implementation is tackled in the right frame of mind.

And perhaps also to provide an opportunity for the plan to be challenged (when plans are still to be finalised) or questions to be asked.

Key things to include

To do a complete job, plans need to be described in terms of ten key stages. These are as follows:

1. Analysis of the current situation (to move forward at all we must understand where we are at the moment: this stage is sometimes referred to as situation analysis), so details need to be spelt out under this heading.

2. The objectives need to be spelt out. Remember objectives are the results you seek to achieve and must be SMART (see page 19 of the Introduction). If they are just vague intentions then the plan is flawed.

3. Creation of options. There is rarely one 'right' way forward so logically various options must be found or created as possible ways ahead.

4. Assessment of the options: all may have pros and cons and an objective assessment of this is a key preliminary to the next stage. Reasons for and against each may sometimes usefully be spelt out (if

only to prevent some people seeing the plan as a second best to another option which they prefer, but for which they do not see the snags).

5. Spell out the chosen strategy (in other words explain what will be done – strategies are the routes to achieving objectives). This is an overview, the next stage takes matters further.

6. Put what will be done in action plan terms (that is spell out the who, what and when of the plan). Often details here below a certain level must wait for more individual briefings.

7. Make implementation procedures clear; this is the first action of putting the plan into effect.

8. Explain the controls that go with the plan (how progress will be monitored) and also how it will be fine-tuned if necessary as the period goes by. Change may range from minor improvements to major rethinks forced by external and unanticipated circumstances.

9. Link what you are saying to the longer term, making it clear that time runs on and, for example, everything does not stop at the end of a particular period or of a financial year.

10. Show the link between the action described and the continuing planning that will ultimately take matters further on (the concept of a 'rolling' plan).

This should encompass any plan or planning process that you have to describe, though for something simpler you may only need a cut down version of this. Some thought ahead of the session about the complexity and how much of the detail needs addressing is clearly sensible.

Dangers to avoid

Think carefully before abbreviating the list above too much and omitting elements that are important to the logic of what is being discussed. Plans that are thought to be ill-judged or not based in reality will not be supported with enthusiasm.

Given the importance of the kind of thing that comes under this heading (and the plan in question might be the complete annual plan for an organisation or department) any lack of clarity is dangerous.

So too is missing out something to address any particular intention that is inherent in the session. For instance, a plan might be explained but, without the question of motivation being addressed, it might still fail because its implementation founders in some way.

Creating a clear structure

Beginning

◆ The first job is to address the complexity and explain carefully to people what you will do, why and how (and maybe mention specifically the level of detail into which you intend to go and the relationship between what you will say and documentation to be available later).

Middle

◆ Like any complex session an agenda needs to be set, used and stuck to.

◆ Be careful about giving people a written plan and then paging through it together. This can be made to work, but it is difficult to stop people reading page ten when you are trying to talk about page five. Perhaps a document can be introduced in the latter part of a meeting once a clear overview has been given.

End

◆ Summary will be a major part of winding up. This is a more difficult art than it may appear when done well by others; it demands careful preparation.

Overall

◆ Plans are to be implemented. However they arise, and they might represent emergency action to retrieve a difficult situation as much as the routine of driving the business forward, so their presentation needs a positive approach and attention to detail.

◆ In terms of manner, a businesslike approach is perhaps the overriding tone to be struck, and your attitude needs to say that you approve and believe in the plan.

Additional dimensions

◆ Plans are important. But they are nothing without people, it is they who make implementation possible. Getting things clear is a serious matter, but unrelieved seriousness can become boring – perhaps you should plan a light moment or two for such a session.

◆ The same is true of participation; think about where you may want involvement or feedback and how you will create that (both as a break in the proceedings or to get other people's views).

Visual aids

◆ The detail here makes visuals of some sort likely to be mandatory, especially where financial plans are a part of the picture or where complex timings and the interrelationships of various stages of a project need spelling out clearly.

◆ For plans of any substance documentation is likely to be involved. If so link the written plan and any slides carefully. They should support each other, yet slides may need individually originating as copying pages from a report and turning them into slides may overwhelm people with inappropriate detail.

Duration

The detail involved will dictate the duration of such a session. With much detail, a great deal to take in, and much or all of it often being new, ensure you take adequate time and also build in adequate breaks.

Speaker's notes

This is a lengthy and detailed session so have adequate guidance and reminders in front of you. If you are highlighting key issues from a detailed written plan, then you may use the plan itself as part of your own running notes (suitably highlighted and annotated). But you may want other guidelines as well, ones that focus only on what you will say and do not allow you to be distracted by the sheer detail of a lengthy planning document.

Useful quotes

'Planning is only anticipating the inevitable, and then taking the credit for it.'   *Overheard*

'Even Emperors can't do it all by themselves.'
                                        Bertolt Brecht

'It is a bad plan that admits of no modification.'
                                        Publilius Syrus

'Planning is like duck shooting – if you aim where the duck is now you will miss the target.'   *Anon*

Delivering bad news

This is never easy; in fact it can be downright difficult. If approached in the right way, however, it may be possible to draw some positive benefit from the occasion. Like the last two sentences bad news needs to be wrapped up, if not with something good, then at least with something less bad. Something may incontrovertibly be bad news; but there are degrees of it and the purpose of talking about it at all may be to mitigate it at least to a degree. It was Lily Tomlin who said *Things are going to get a lot worse before they get worse,* thus illustrating an attitude that you should try to be at pains to avoid.

Maximising the opportunity

Informing people of the situation is an objective, but the opportunities that accompany it are several:

◆ To prevent rumours (perhaps telling a worse tale than the true one) starting; this makes an immediate and important point – putting off telling bad news is almost always going to make a bad situation worse. It is something to address promptly.

◆ To soften the blow, if that is possible.

◆ To spell out any action resulting from whatever the bad news is.

◆ Spell out compensating points or action and in so doing affect the response to both what is happening and what is being done about it.

To illustrate the last point let us consider a situation in which there must be redundancies. This is a real blow for those people being made redundant and may make others fearful. A good package and assistance for those leaving helps them and will be seen by others as a sign of a caring management; the signals both the action and the response to it send may be helpful in the aftermath of whatever has caused the problem.

Key things to include

The news, clearly described and without fudging the issue.

The resulting action, including any designed to compensate for what has happened (like the good redundancy package and arrangements).

Background and explanation; together with any compensating factors. For example a sales downturn might lead to redundancies, but advancing new product launch plans that might, in time, increase sales again and be a step towards retrieving the situation may mitigate to a degree.

Many circumstances make it worthwhile to describe the current situation even in the early moments after whatever it is that is bad has occurred. Is management on top of the situation? Is a positive response in train? Are steps being taken to stop things getting worse?

Individual responsibilities may need highlighting. If some individual was clearly to blame and action can be described as already having been taken (they have been fired, suspended, whatever) then this may make other people feel better.

Everything must be dealt with evident realism. It is not possible to wind the clock back. What has happened has happened, and what happens next is what matters and how that is approached will affect people as much as the original problem.

Dangers to avoid

If the news is bad and yet is announced without any apology, explanation or even the beginnings of action designed to compensate then the danger is that the organisation – or its management (or you) – will appear uncaring or incompetent. Any such feelings will make a bad situation worse.

If the person announcing the news is at pains to distance themselves from the blame this must be done carefully and it must be credible. Similarly if blame seems to be being shifted elsewhere inappropriately then this will be resented.

Creating a clear structure

Beginning

◆ Start with a bald announcement (rumour may in any case be ahead of you), then spell out the agenda for the session so that the response seems sensible.

◆ If there are likely to be obvious fears that you can dispel, then do so early on as otherwise worrying about them will prevent people listening as carefully as you no doubt want.

◆ Make it clear how questions will be handled, and when, and what else is set up to explain further – *Hold questions for the moment until I have spelt out the facts, then we can take any point you want to raise, though it is already arranged that those affected can have a one to one session with their immediate manager before the end of the day.*

Middle

◆ Once the agenda is spelt out for the main part of the session stick to it, and work through the details systematically.

◆ Remind people if necessary how questions will be handled and keep these in place so that they enhance, rather than disrupt, the structure you have decided upon.

End

Two things predominate here (in addition to any necessary summary):

- A note of apology or sympathy (see next section).

- Action for the future and, if possible, a positive end (though do not contrive it, if nothing positive can be said at this stage do not pretend otherwise).

Overall
- A note of apology or sympathy may need to be evident throughout the process. If so make it sincere and remember that, as a manager, you speak for the organisation: *I am sorry* is what is necessary (though you may have no fault in the matter) and *We are sorry* only aggravates (after all, who is 'we' exactly?).

- In terms of manner, you need to combine the note of sympathy, even apology, referred to above with a businesslike approach to what follows.

- The tone may be serious, even sombre, but the tone needs to balance this with some resolution and, if possible, certainty. Facts must be straight and clear, plans seem sensible even if necessarily not long considered. Some bad news is expected, there has been some warning or it reflects an ever-present hazard. If so there may be contingency plans in place. This fact may need emphasising and the readiness it describes may give confidence about a positive final outcome being possible.

Additional dimensions
- There may be things that can be learnt from what

has happened; however, think carefully about how much you say about this – it may often be dealt with as a second stage

◆ Some bad news could repeat and part of what needs to be done is to demonstrate what can be done to prevent a repeat (and perhaps how people in the audience can help prevent something similar happening again).

Visual aids

◆ A short lead time may prevent anything much being done here, though if something would clearly be useful then efforts should be made to make it possible.

◆ If nothing is available then allow for it, for example taking more care or time (or both) to explain something that a slide would normally make clear more easily.

◆ If something is necessary or helpful, consider simple ways – a flip chart perhaps – rather than using nothing just because there is not time or opportunity to create proper slides.

Duration

The duration needs to do justice to the situation, and the impression must not be given that brevity is designed to dispatch the matter in inappropriately short order, or avoid going into details or giving people the opportunity to ask questions.

Indeed it is the kind of session where actually saying something like *I will take as long as you want to give you all the detail you want* may be appreciated and thus recommended.

Speaker's notes
Such a session (as others) may be summoned at short notice and any preparation time may be at a premium. Resist the temptation to skimp getting yourself organised. Burn the midnight oil, postpone a meeting but be sure you put yourself in a position to run this with confidence (of presenting the facts if not of solving everything outstanding).

Your notes must be sufficient to make this possible.

Useful quotes
'Bad news travels fast.'   *Proverb*

'When sorrows come/They come not in single spies/ But in battalions!'   *William Shakespeare*

'The rule is, jam tomorrow and jam yesterday – but never jam today.'   *Lewis Carroll*

Dealing with statistics

Another topic looks at talking about money and there is certainly a crossover here, but it is worth looking at certain specifics of statistics. They are as apt to confuse as to illuminate. The very formality of statistically based figures, percentages and the like, gives them authority. Yet ... there is a story of a man frightened of flying, his fears made worse by imagining a bomb on board. The odds were considerably against, but – he calculated – the odds against there being *two* bombs on board were astronomical; so he always took one with him. This is not, of course, quite how statistics work.

Unless such figures are used with precision, and accompanied by suitable explanation, they may not just be ineffective, they may confuse and create the reverse of the impact they are designed to produce.

Maximising the opportunity

The opportunity is to make a point, perhaps a strong or dramatic one, by making the basis of something clear in terms of the figures involved.

It is only an opportunity if the way the figures are used is understood and thus able to make the chosen point.

An additional opportunity here is to score points by making what people expect to be complicated be found to be (easily) understandable. Psychologists talk about what they call 'cognitive cost' to describe the relative difficulty of something. A concept made clear to many people by saying that the instruction to your video recorder almost certainly has a high cognitive cost! Offer them a low one and they love it.

It may be that there is a good reason to choose a way of presenting statistics that exaggerate a good picture, but care is needed here and it is all too easy for an inappropriately exaggerated statement to come back to haunt you.

Key things to include

To maximise the effectiveness of statistics, indeed any complex figures, you should:

◆ Make the principles you will use clear, for example always describing a percentage as a percentage *of* something else (something specific).

◆ State the figures clearly and allow a moment's thinking time for them to 'sink in'.

◆ Check understanding if necessary – *All clear?* – or ask a question to verify that understanding exists (remembering that people do not want to look stupid by asking what might seem to be silly questions).

◆ Illustrate wherever possible (slides are very useful here) and put things in the simplest possible form, for example a pie chart.

◆ Link the figures clearly to the point you are making (explaining the link as you do so) – *So, if the increase is only 3% and we are aiming at five – that leaves us with a shortfall of 2% and that represents £X thousand of additional sales to make.*

◆ If action flows from the point then make what that is clear too.

Dangers to avoid

Assuming that your figures are accurate (are they?) beware of any kind of vagueness. An example, para-phrased from the excellent book *Innumeracy* (John Allen Paulus: Penguin), shows just how misleading (and worrying in this case) loose representation of statistics can be. A doctor is quoted, who in a matter of a few minutes, tells a patient their operation has only a one in a million risk associated with it, then that it is 99% safe and finally that it 'usually went quite well'. I think I would have wanted to know which!

More specific dangers include allowing or inadvertently encouraging:

◆ *Inappropriate association of percentages:* for instance a product reduced in price by 40% and then again by another 40% has been reduced by a total of 64% (not 80% – you cannot add percentages in that way).

◆ *The vague use of 'average':* there is, for instance a difference between the 'median' (the figure mid way through a group of numbers, and the 'mode' (the value that occurs most often in a group, and the 'average' (the number found by adding all the numbers in a group and dividing by the number of numbers in a set) – yet all may be called an 'average' if no precision is employed.

◆ *Maximising the percentage number:* as in a case where it is said something (say), a toothpaste's ability to reduce cavities is 200%. Sounds impressive and perhaps only means that it reduces them by 30% compared with a rival brand's 10% (the 30% reduction is a 200% increase of the 10% reduction). A typical case of tweaking figures to produce something impressive-sounding and destroying meaning – and credibility? – at the same time.

◆ *Adding percentages:* in manufacturing, if eight components rise in price by 5% then the total price rise is just 5%, not eight times that – 40%.

Even the wrong choice of one word may negate what you are trying to do. Forecasts are, by definition, only estimates. It is wrong to say something is estimated as 10.2456%. The four figures of decimals are likely irrelevant, adding a misleading feeling of accuracy to what needs to be considered as a ball park figure. Computers will do calculations automatically and it is then all too easy just to read off what they say, however inappropriate.

This list can only give the flavour of what to look out for here – resolve to proceed with care whenever statistics must be presented.

Perhaps obvious, but any hint of a disjointed presentation the *And another thing* approach – will quickly dilute impact.

Creating a clear structure

Content is most likely not 'just statistics' so structure will likely need to be for the overall topic. That said, with statistics in mind, remember the following:

Beginning

◆ It may be worth mentioning the need for statistics, what you are using them for – and how you will make them clear – before getting into the figures.

◆ Make it clear what handouts people will get, you do not want them spending time trying to write everything down if they will receive a summary.

◆ That said a punchy start and a clear agenda are as important here as elsewhere.

Middle

◆ Take one point at a time and do not move on until it seems to be accepted.

◆ Maintain an overall, and well explained, logic throughout the session.

End

◆ Summary may be important to highlight any key figures again.

◆ The topic will dictate other aspects of the conclusion (an action linked ending?).

◆ If a written résumé of the statistical detail can be obtained say so.

Overall

◆ Clarity first, foremost and throughout should be the watchword here. Take one point at a time and never be overoptimistic about your audience's ability to take in this kind of information (equally I guess one should be careful of treating those with a high degree of numeracy like a six year old, but the prime danger is the reverse).

◆ Figures can be dry and may seem dull, so create an element of interest (even of levity) where possible; or simply take a break.

◆ In terms of manner, you must make it interesting and also appear businesslike and thorough in the way you handle the details; as describing statistics is not an end in itself, your manner needs to reflect the overall purpose of the session in which they play a part.

Additional dimensions

◆ Be especially careful if figures are monitored

regularly (as happens with organisation financial results) and make sure that the starting point – last month's statement or whatever – is clear before moving on.

◆ Remember that retention of the detail of figures can be difficult, so use handouts and summaries where necessary to create a permanent record.

Visual aids
◆ These are likely to be a great help, however do not give all your attention to them (looking at a screen and not your audience, for example).

◆ Find ways of getting everyone to be able to focus quickly on the same thing – *Look at the graph and follow the red line* (make sure you choose colours that contrast and are easily seen and differentiated).

◆ Use slides that present only the information you want, not from which you highlight one thing and ignore others; saying *Ignore the rest just look at* is very unsatisfying and people just wonder what they are missing.

Duration

As with discussion of money (and it may be worth reading Topic Talking about Money in conjunction with this one) allow time to do a thorough job and achieve a real understanding.

Speaker's notes

Remember that hesitancy – *Let me see, that's 10%, no – sorry – it's 12%* – may easily be read as uncertainty and destroy any conviction that your message may be intended to carry. So make sure that what you have in front of you is clear, legible and that you can link easily to your next slide and keep the message progressing steadily.

Useful quotes

'There are three kinds of lies – lies, damned lies and statistics.'   *Benjamin Disraeli*

'He uses statistics like a drunken man uses lamp posts – for support rather than illumination.'
Andrew Lang

'Facts speak louder than statistics.'
Geoffrey Streatfield

'Five out of every three people can't work out fractions.'   *Ken Dodd*

'I have yet to see any problem, however complicated, which when looked at in the right way, did not become still more complicated.'   *Poul Anderson*

Calling for action

Many a presentation might have a call for action inherent within it. Nevertheless the core aspects of getting a commitment to action are worth a word in their own right. It is no longer the case (if it ever were) that a manager can simply say *Do this* and people will. Real commitment and something being done properly and perhaps with enthusiasm demands more. You must put over a message that is understood, that is accepted and which prompts agreement to act (and perhaps also acts to prompt rejecting other options).

Maximising the opportunity

The task is to prompt action. Opportunity? Apart from just getting the action you want under way, the opportunity is to influence the attitude of people as they take action. It may be done, but done grudgingly; or done better and found motivational.

Key things to include

Much here will go with the topic, beyond that:

◆ Make *exactly* what needs to be done clear. This means thinking about the description beforehand so that it can be precisely and succinctly stated with no *sort of*s or other evidence of lack of thinking it through audible.

◆ Use some of the time to *explain* the background and *why* something needs to be done and what the *results will be* (including how the people themselves will be affected).

◆ Provide evidence of what you say if it is necessary to really persuade people to a point of view.

◆ Address in parallel the question of motivation: what will make this action interesting, rewarding or fun to take? Spell that out too.

◆ Summarise the *who*, *what* and *when* elements of the action without any ambiguity.

Dangers to avoid

The worst thing is to try to announce action too early, before it is thoroughly worked out. A plan begins to emerge, then so do problems or unresolved details, and the end result is that the whole thing appears as if people are being asked to take a shot in the dark.

Any kind of lack of precision where the reverse of this would be expected can dilute the effect of the whole.

If authority to insist on action is needed, then the message will suffer if it comes over without the necessary 'weight'.

Be careful of deadlines. Will they be considered possible? Reasonable? How will hitting them affect other planned activity? Just announcing them if they need explanation or justification can antagonise.

Creating a clear structure

Beginning

◆ As usual clarity of purpose is important, so too may be injecting a little excitement about what is to be done (it can be a challenge but still represent an attractive thing to do).

◆ Deal with the detail: for example announcing that a note will be circulated to summarise dates and other details that might otherwise keep people scribbling throughout the session.

Middle

◆ The action plan element will probably dictate the structure. One thing at a time and an overall 'shape' spelt out ahead of going into detail will keep the session manageable – for you and the audience.

End

◆ The end must leave no loose ends and demands a clear summary.

◆ Do not revisit everything, and if a lot of detail has been gone through link it to a clear description of what follows (a summary memo, further meetings and so on).

Overall

◆ The action required dictates the style here, initial statements should make clear that action is necessary and the explanation and detail that follows must be seen in the context of getting it right and achieving the planned goals.

◆ In terms of manner, again this needs to be a businesslike session; but a few human touches will bring it to life – for example, a few light touches ahead of a busy period of implementation may be both appropriate and be used to add to the injunction to act.

Additional dimensions

◆ The focus here is important. With detail to be gone through and action to get right, it is usually best not to allow the confusion made possible by any digression or doubling up of intention; an action session should be an action session, no more, no less.

Visual aids

◆ The key specific thing here is to use visuals to reinforce the detail that it is necessary to get over, and perhaps also speed up the process and avoid anything that smacks of over-engineering.

Duration

If a session is to spell out action and ensure that it

happens, then sufficient time must be spent to achieve this. If adopting the action is seen as straightforward and the session makes too much of a meal of it this may be resented and the message diluted as a result. At worst, too elaborate a briefing may be seen as patronising.

Speaker's notes

What is necessary will depend mostly on the topic and the detail involved. One straightforward action may need only a few words as a checklist to put over. A complex series of actions demands clarity of detail in your material as a prerequisite to achieving clarity in putting it over.

Useful quotes

'Never confuse activity with achievement.'   *Anon*

'Ninety percent of success is turning up.'
Woody Allen

'Knowledge fuelled by emotion equals action.'
Jim Rohn

'Ready, aim, fire is always the best order in which to do things.'   *Anon*

Matching tasks and competencies

Here we might link with other topics (Sounding a warning, and Announcing something new, for instance), the occasion when something demands an extension to people's competencies. A new system, way of working or changed demands in the market place may all demand not simply different action by people but that things are done in a way that demands new skills.

There is no criticism involved here. We are talking about additional skills not about something done badly that must be improved. For example, people may need to acquire the ability to make presentations, to handle customer enquires at a computer screen instead of just on the telephone or deploy new information in discussing a new product or changed product application.

Training may be necessary; here we are not talking about conducting the training but explaining to people that it will be necessary.

Maximising the opportunity

Let us be clear. Operationally this kind of situation may be annoying, you have to upgrade or add to people's skills before things can run on as you wish. On the other hand, it is normal – we live in dynamic times; it would be odd if nothing ever needed changing in this way. The pressure for this kind of thing may be technological, come from competitive changes, or be prompted by changing customer requirements – or more.

The opportunity is twofold:

◆ First, it is to secure the operational methods and standards required.

◆ Secondly, it is an opportunity to develop and motivate people.

The first of these needs no comment here, operational standards must be kept up to date; ultimately it is a matter of survival. The second, however, is worth dwelling on for a moment. Most people, if they must work, want to draw some satisfaction from it. Most want their work to be interesting (they want job satisfaction), and this means that, while they may resist change – at least to begin with – they do not want to do exactly the same job repetitively for ever. There is all the difference in the world between five years' experience and one year's experience repeated five times. Most people want the former.

Surveys in management magazines often ask what people want of managers. All sorts of things get listed (that they are fair, good listeners and that they consult their staff), but one thing always features high. People want to work for people who allow – encourage – them to develop and expand what they do; in effect to learn.

The opportunity here is a significant one to set people up for learning in a way that makes that go well and which, in turn, allows operational matters to be improved.

Key things to include

An explanation of *what* is required and *why* (one that makes it clear that this is a natural development, not a criticism of past performance – if criticism *is* necessary then that is another matter – see Issuing a reprimand).

A description of it both in personal terms – development, job satisfaction and progress – as well as of the operational side.

Chapter and verse on what will be done, set out in a way that encourages, enthuses and removes any fears that may be anticipated (for example, presentations skills training might involve making presentations and people might find this a daunting thing to do in front of colleagues).

Dangers to avoid

The key danger is allowing the need for something to be seen as a reflection on people's past performance, allowing them to take what is to be done as a criticism.

There is also the danger that while people take the change in the right spirit, they are also fearful of actually being able to make the improvement involved – *I'll never be able to do that!* If there are some people who may *not* actually be able to cope then this will need dealing with separately.

Overselling it – *This incredible opportunity* – will sound patronising and do more harm than good.

Creating a clear structure

Beginning

◆ Start on a positive note and make it clear that you are talking about the impact and implications on individuals as well as more broadly on the organisation.

◆ In setting an agenda, separate the opportunity from the detail of what must be done and the action to be taken.

Middle

◆ Arrange the different matters here so as to combine a logical approach with something that allows you to present the whole thing in a manner that relates to people's motivation.

◆ Include sufficient information about why as well as what, give any necessary background and stress the results that all this makes possible.

◆ Go through the detailed content in a sequence that makes good sense from both these points of view, perhaps chronologically – that is taking the changes first, the advantages of change, then what will be done and the detail of how, and how to that affects individuals.

End

◆ Summarise as the detail necessitates, refer to further action (course dates being issued in writing, perhaps) and conclude on a positive note – again making it clear that people are being presented with an opportunity.

Overall

◆ Pitching what you say at the right level is important here. It is unlikely to be routine, and it may be a mistake to describe it as the biggest opportunity ever. The overall feel is perhaps best dictated by the nature of the change and what produces the need for it.

◆ It must always seem like well-considered action.

◆ In terms of manner, it needs a positive and enthusiastic approach – remember that enthusiasm can be infectious – coupled with a businesslike approach to the core matters in hand.

Additional dimensions

◆ Consider where all this leads. Does it imply permanent change to job responsibilities and job descriptions (and rewards)? Does it change any other details, for example supervision or management control systems, and do such aspects need announcing? Is there an opportunity for further incentives, for example a prize for whoever does best in the subsequent training? Think widely before shutting down on the content you will include in such a session. Some things here may follow later than an initial announcement, but may usefully be hinted at in this session.

Visual aids
◆ Normal considerations apply here.

◆ If a formal course follows then it may be possible to use some of the materials that will be used in that as a sort of 'taster'.

Duration
People should see this as an interesting session, and indeed it is both important and interesting. So therefore it should not be necessary to curtail it fiercely. The content and topic will naturally dictate the duration.

Speaker's notes
These can be designed to fit the amount of detail and the precision with which the overall topic needs to be dealt. Fit in any material from a subsequent course carefully, especially if you are only highlighting certain things from the whole.

Useful quotes

'There is no shortcut to any place worth going.'

Beverly Sills

'When you're through changing, you're through. Change is a process, not a destination.'

Robert Kriegel and David Brandt

'It is what you learn after you know it all that counts.'

John Wooden

'Knowledge advances by steps, and not by leaps.'

Lord Macaulay

Announcing results

People like feedback about how things are going, and particularly about how their bit is going and also how it is contributing to the whole. Natural enough – after all who would enjoy a football match if there was no one keeping score? So, this may be a regular one to undertake – indeed remember that the time scale on which you report to people should be based, in part at least, on their perceptions. Probably the rule should be sooner rather than later (though obviously some results are definitive such as those representing the financial year).

Maximising the opportunity

At one level the intention is simply to keep people well informed; and there is nothing wrong with that, indeed people like it. Given the continuity involved, the information about *how well have we done so far* links to the future, highlighting also what must be done next in the way that half year results highlight the following six months.

In addition, the results may:

◆ Reward people, giving a sense of achievement and thus acting to motivate (indeed they may link to tangible rewards like bonuses or commission).

◆ Act as an incentive and – linked to other action – encourage future efforts and make it more likely that subsequent targets are hit.

◆ Highlight failure, large or small, and act to admonish people for it. Though it should be said, by way of reminder, that sticks work best in parallel with carrots.

Information about results may also influence actions, as record sales leading to an out of stock situation on a particular product leads to different action in handling customer orders and enquiries – at least for a while.

Key things to include

What you say will depend on the actual circumstances – whether results are good or bad. That said, and using positive results as the example, you need to:

Decide and describe the period you will discuss, for example how far back do you need to look to get things in perspective? (Be careful to compare like with like – a great improvement may appear only because of a comparison with a period of famine.)

◆ Make the results clear, being especially careful with financial figures and other statistics (see page 80).

◆ Make the figures live, or even exciting, for example by making interesting comparisons or descriptive analogies – *The amount of product shipped this week would cover ten football pitches.*

◆ If appropriate, give credit where credit is due and make it personal if this is merited.

◆ Look ahead, whether this is a major or minor part of your overall intentions.

Dangers to avoid

Blinding people with science – for example using large figures that have no meaning to people at the level at which you are discussing matters.

Failing to relate the overall situation to particular matters within, say, one individual department allowing it all to seem somewhat academic.

Going through the motions but not using the opportunity to link to personal issues or future action.

There may be negative points to be made if results are poor, and if so you need to do so. But do not overdo this, after all you cannot wind the clock back and the only task now faced is to make things better in future. The balance here may be important.

Creating a clear structure

Beginning

◆ With several possibilities in terms of overall intention, be clear at the start about what it is you are going to do – *With excellent results in the last month, I'll first have a look at what we have done, see if I can ferret out what made this possible, and then look ahead. We do not want to let one good month end up allowing us to rest on our laurels.*

Middle

◆ Take one point at a time.

◆ Take time to allow you to bring complex matters to life.

◆ Separate past, present and future and make sure that, if you have multiple intentions, each is given the attention it deserves.

End

◆ This is another topic where complexity and figures may make a clear summary necessary.

◆ Touch again on any personal mentions or thanks that are necessary.

◆ End by looking ahead, on a positive note and with any action points for the future clearly spelt out.

Overall

◆ If results are positive this should be a motivational occasion. If not you may still need to motivate and must do so by looking ahead.

◆ In terms of manner, this must follow the nature of the results and may, on occasion need a note of sobriety, but ultimately looking ahead must take the spotlight and that needs a positive tone.

Additional dimensions
◆ The key overlap here is with the future. You need to take a view of what can usefully be said about results to date using that as a springboard to a variety of things you might want to say about the future.

Visual aids
◆ Use what is necessary to match the complexity of any details or figures involved, and use graphs and other such devices to ensure clarity.

Duration

This can vary a good deal, some results deserve no more than a minute or two in a departmental meeting, others are a major issue deserving their own meeting or a major section of an annual review.

Speaker's notes

The same thing applies here as to any situation where detail, and figures, are involved – be careful to have the right details clear and in front of you.

Useful quotes

'Failure is the opportunity to begin again more intelligently.'
Henry Ford

'Nothing recedes like success.'   *Walter Winchell*

'It is as hard to stay on top as it is to get there.'
Hugh Cudlipp

'Success requires no apologies; failure permits no alibis.'
Anon

Addressing a coming challenge

The topic here implies something that may be prompted by something negative (the need to make up for some difficulty or failure), or by something positive (tackling something that is best described as an opportunity – but which will present some difficulty). The difficulty may be inherent because of something complex or new, perhaps. Or the task may be made difficult by something else, a tight deadline, say.

Maximising the opportunity

The opportunity, indeed the task, is first to inform. Secondly, to specify the task and to do so in a way that helps make it seem possible. Thirdly, to motivate people to want to do or even to view it as fun.

Key things to include

First make clear what the challenge is and then, in an organised way, set out why it is necessary, how it can be done and link it to any action plan that is also necessary.

Where appropriate, make it sound interesting and exciting. People like a challenge, certainly they like tackling one and succeeding – it produces a sense of achievement and may link to that being recognised in some way, which they like even more. There is evidence that people like, and respond best to, a big challenge – one worthy of the name.

Dangers to avoid

Overusing the term, making a mountain out of what is not even much of a molehill will not interest people, much less get them fired up to do something.

Projecting a lack of confidence that makes what needs to be done sound unreasonable or impossible.

Using a dismissive *It's no problem* or *Of course you can do it* approach without saying anything about *how* success will be achieved and *why*, therefore, it is possible.

Creating a clear structure

Beginning

◆ Define the challenge and begin to look beyond just the sheer difficulty involved as soon as possible

◆ Set out an agenda in a way that makes it clear that you will talk about how it is possible, indeed that you believe that it is.

Middle

◆ As ever, a logical approach is needed here, do not let enthusiasm overpower organisation.

◆ The detailed structure will come from the nature of the challenge and the extent to which there is a detailed action plan to be gone through describing what must be done (that aspect is dealt with elsewhere).

End

◆ There is only one place to end and that is on a note of belief in success, which may need to combine several different factors – *It is difficult* (but we will do it), *We know how to tackle it* (action plans), *Doing it will* (results), and *It might even be fun.*

Overall

◆ This needs a businesslike approach that submerges the difficulty in a sheer weight of can-do factors both motivational and practical. Whilst the challenge should be accepted and not hidden, the session is to persuade people that it is possible to get to grips with what must be done and make it possible.

◆ In terms of manner, three things are key – it should be positive, positive and positive.

Additional dimensions

◆ The major link here is between describing the challenge and persuading people that the task it represents can be successfully accomplished, and spelling out the details of how it can be done which adds a whole separate dimension to the session.

◆ Consider too whether there needs to be some tangible incentive linked to the task designed to motivate, make it more interesting and help ensure that it does get done successfully.

♦ Given the weight of the matter, and the motivational aspect running in parallel with it, unrelenting seriousness may be wrong and an occasional light touch can help the session along.

Visual aids

♦ Visuals that *illustrate* tackling a challenge successfully may be helpful, but too many or trite things along these lines may well be seen as patronising.

Duration

This topic may link to setting out a plan of action (see page 150) and if this is the case then it may take a little time. Time spent at this stage that results in something being done right and that, in turn, produces a successful outcome is much to be preferred over time spent to rescue a difficult situation that is progressing badly.

Speaker's notes

This area, like others, will be influenced by the complexity of the whole session, and whether it includes an action plan or not. A plethora of detail needs more organising and more of an aide memoire to help it get delivered in the right way.

Useful quotes

'If you think you can, you can. And if you think you can't, you're right.'   *Mary Kay Ash*

'The word impossible is not in my dictionary.'
Napoleon Bonaparte

'Champions keep playing until they get it right.'
Billie Jean King

'Success is not the result of spontaneous combustion. You must first set fire to yourself.'   *Fred Shero*

Mission accomplished

People hate feeling ignored or taken for granted. They also hate being kept in the dark, so sessions that acknowledge progress and completion of whatever work is being done are always valuable. Some may have a kind of *So far so good* brief, some overlap with a *Well done*. The key thing reviewed here is the acknowledgement of work being completed or of a significant stage being reached.

Regularly done this kind of session need not take long and can be made informative and useful; and is appreciated.

Maximising the opportunity

The opportunity is primarily one of information. Such sessions keep people posted, and this is valuable in its own right and much better than the alternative of their feeling neglected.

It is also an opportunity to:

◆ Praise and motivate, to acknowledge what has been done to date and work on ensuring that the remainder of a task is completed satisfactorily.

◆ Fine-tune action. For example, to speed something up aiming for completion ahead of an original deadline or add something, perhaps to achieve greater quality.

◆ Address shortfalls. Finishing stage one late may still be an achievement and if more remains to be done then a 'mission accomplished' approach to moving ahead may still be relevant.

◆ Focus on an individual contribution.

Key things to include

A clear *Well done* (and consider the extent of this *I must say* or *Everyone thinks* or *The M.D. asked me to add his congratulations* – or maybe they should be there!).

If some people are unaware of it describe what was done and why it was a challenge.

In addition, you may want to talk about:

◆ How something was done.

◆ Lessons learnt from doing it.

◆ How different people played their part.

◆ Particular, perhaps unexpected, hazards overcome along the way.

◆ The results now occurring or in prospect.

Dangers to avoid

Any apparent lack of sincerity or going through the motions will negate a session intended to thank and acknowledge achievement.

Similarly the achievement must be real; if minor things are addressed in a way that exaggerates their importance, perhaps just to find an opportunity to motivate, then it will devalue real achievement.

Creating a clear structure

Beginning

◆ Make the congratulatory nature of the session immediately apparent.

◆ Then set out the extent of the statement or review that follows, as the duration and extent may vary.

Middle

◆ Think about the extent of your comments – the opportunities referred to above – and order them appropriately in a way that gives pride of place to the key issues and achievements and fits best with your overall intention.

◆ Keep ongoing comment, for instance about what happens next, separate from talk about what has been done.

End

◆ Whatever else is necessary to summarise and pull together loose ends, always end back on the good things and the congratulations.

Overall

◆ In terms of manner, this should be businesslike and

perhaps enthusiastic, congratulatory and done in a way that expresses gratitude where appropriate (to both the team and to individuals).

Additional dimensions
◆ This is a topic that may well have multiple intentions and examples of such are made clear under Maximising the opportunities above.

Visual aids
◆ Unless such a session is extended to overlap with other topics or used as much to set the scene for the next stage of something as to look back, then visual aids are probably not necessary.

Duration
There can be short and long versions of this. The short version may do little more than acknowledge the completion of something. Longer sessions will be made so primarily by also setting out what comes next. At the short end it must be sufficiently long to give the matter unequivocal importance.

Speaker's notes
Congratulations alone may not need much documenting, though you need to be careful to get facts, times and names right. Longer sessions will need a greater amount of detail in front of you.

Useful quotes

'If at first you don't succeed, try, try again. Then quit. No use being a damn fool about it.'

W. C. Fields

'Good luck is the reason for other people's success.'

Anon

'Whatever doesn't kill you, makes you stronger.'

Marlon Brando

'The only place where success comes before work is in the dictionary.'   *Vidal Sassoon*

Introducing a training session

As a trainer I am always amazed at how rarely managers introduce the in-company courses that I conduct. I am also usually struck by just how useful it is when they do so. Any training is expensive in terms of both time and money. You want to make the most of it. Whether a course is conducted by an outside consultant, or by another manager or specialist such as a training manager, you should always take advantage of the opportunity this presents.

Maximising the opportunity

There are several opportunities to:

◆ Demonstrate management's commitment to training in general and one programme in particular.

◆ Stress the practical importance of training, this course and this topic.

◆ Motivate people and comment on the career value of training.

◆ Link to current factors (how a greater skill in something will help a particular project).

◆ Mention the luxury (I think that is the right word) of being able to take time to step back from operational pressures and really *think* about what creates the level of performance desired.

◆ Reassure, if necessary, regarding any aspect of the training that may worry participants.

Key things to include

First, there may be things to be said about training overall: its importance, how specifically past training has produced tangible change or results, future plans or a request for ideas, for instance.

Secondly, you want to link comments to the particular course in question. You might comment on:

◆ The subject of the training, why it is important and how it helps people and processes.

◆ The people on the course, what they do and how the training will help them.

◆ The tasks people on the course deal with and how training links to that.

◆ The nature of the training – for example the degree of participation involved, how that will work and the opportunity it provides.

◆ Both short and longer term implications of what is going on.

In addition, there may be negative things to comment on; perhaps a problem of some sort has prompted the course. These may need mentioning, but do *not* let them overpower an overall positive feel just as the course starts.

Anecdotes and experiences that illustrate just how training can influence things may well be useful.

It may be useful to confer with the course tutor and see if you can deal with any matters ahead of the course actually starting. For example, getting some of the administrative matters out of the way allows a more punchy start to the 'course proper'.

Finally, it may be your role to introduce the tutor.

Dangers to avoid

The things that will most quickly negate the good that can be done here are if:

◆ Your speech is seen only as a gesture (something that *should* be done).

◆ You, as a more senior manager, are seen as distanced and seem not to understand 'what it is like at the coal face'.

◆ People feel you should be there with them! So, if you are, say, the worst time manager in the organisation resist the temptation to introduce a time management course, but not attend it (and if you do introduce a time management course – start on, and stick to, time!).

Creating a clear structure

Beginning

◆ Say why you are there (participants may be expecting only the trainer) and if you do not know people then introduce yourself.

◆ Strike a positive note early on.

◆ Say what your purpose is and make it clear you are not taking over the programme.

Middle

◆ Make the various, and perhaps disparate, points (see Key things to include above) in a logical way and stick to your stated purpose and agenda.

End

◆ Stick to your alloted (stated?) time.

◆ Whatever negative factors may be around (the course might be designed to correct a weakness) finish on an enthusiastic and constructive note.

Overall

◆ The overall balance should almost certainly be positive.

◆ Training can do only three things. It can impart knowledge, develop skills or change attitudes. These, and the link between the topic of the course and operational activity, are the places for the focus of this kind of session.

◆ In terms of manner, what works best here is a mix
of a businesslike manner and enthusiasm.

Additional dimensions

◆ What you say at the start of a training programme
might be used to set up a secondary session. Thus
you would join the group again at the end of the
course. At that time, as people mix informally, there
is a classic opportunity to canvass feedback about
the course and opinions about wider matters. This
is an example of the useful technique (and a phrase
coined in the classic book *In Search of Excellence*) –
Management By Walking About (MBWA).

Visual aids

◆ Are only likely to be needed if you do more than
introduce and start to get into the course content. If
so you might use slides from the course material.

◆ Be careful not to use anything that looks shabby
compared with what will be used on the
programme.

Duration

Do not outstay your welcome, nor eat into the tutor's
time (or what they will say!) and agree your timing with
the tutor.

Speaker's notes

These should not be elaborate. If you are trying to be

succinct, and you probably are, then any notes must help achieve just that.

Useful quotes

'In theory there is no difference between theory and practice. In practice there is.' *Yogi Berra*

'For goodness sake, don't ask me if you can attend an assertiveness training course – just go and register.' *Overheard*

'Sending men to war without training is like abandoning them.' *Confucius*

'First it was: "Training? No one does any training in retail". Then we progressed to: "What if I train my staff and they leave?" To which the only response is: "What if you don't train them – and they stay?" ' *Debra Templar*

Afterword

'Talking and eloquence are not the same: to speak, and to speak well, are two things.'

Ben Johnson

The whole concept of this book – a focus on key issues and particular tasks – precludes an elaborate summary. So the following does not attempt to be comprehensive, rather just to touch on certain key issues with an eye on increasing the likelihood of your presentations getting better and better:

Consider the alternatives: dangers or opportunities

The dangers of poor presentations do not need reiterating again in detail. It is enough to say that they have both business elements – not meeting your objectives or achieving what you want in terms of results and actions – and personal ones – which range from feeling mildly inadequate to seeing a rapid death as preferable to continuing to speak for another moment.

Both are to be avoided.

The incentives to do so are very real. Presentational skills provide opportunities, and can sometimes do so in a major way. Once acquired these skills can help you in your job, in your career and in achieving things large and small in either the long or short term; or in any or all of these ways.

So acquiring them is worth working at and, although you may not achieve the standard you want instantly or without some effort, remember the old saying: opportunities often come disguised – as hard work. In fact, you may quickly turn in a workmanlike standard – and be surprised at just what you can in fact achieve.

Deal with the negatives

Accept that – for whatever reason – most people seem to anticipate difficulty with presentations. Accept also that there are many disparate matters that can easily conspire to make presenting effectively more difficult. But work to defuse such factors. The balance analogy referred to earlier is a good one. So too is the idea of mental reach. Your mind can only stretch itself around so many things at once (at least mine can!). It is a bit like a juggler with a number of balls in the air at the same time: faults – even tiny ones – quickly add up and they may find themselves not just dropping one ball, but several or, at worst, them all.

Similarly, if a part of your mind is busy thinking, say, *what do I do with my hands? – my hands are so awkward – everyone is noticing,* then there is a little less of it available to focus on delivering an appropriate message in the right way. So, every problem or potential problem that you deal with – *I'm comfortable with one hand on the lectern and the other holding a pen* – in whatever way, reduces the feeling of pressure of trying to concentrate on a dozen things at once and *yet still* deliver the presentation.

The first step to success here is simply the adoption of a way of approaching this. That leads to dealing with problems one by one until they are insufficient to dilute in any serious way what you are trying to do. Of course, you cannot reduce them completely. Certainly few people ever get over some feeling of nervousness, particularly as they start to speak; indeed many would say a little apprehension at that stage is a good thing – the adrenaline it produces is necessary to the job to be done. If the feeling still worries you at least label it positively: I once heard one speaker saying he never had nerves, but admitted to a feeling of what he called 'creative apprehension'.

Understand the process

Not only was it said earlier that presentation deserved some study, but at this point (assuming you have read through to here from the beginning!) you have done some. There may be more to do, but certainly you will have been exposed to many of the fundamental principles that make for good presenting. Knowledge of these factors gives you something to aim for. If you understand the power of a dramatic pause, say, and how to hold it long enough to create the effect you want, then there is more chance of your not only trying it, but deploying it successfully. So too is it with other techniques and tricks of the trade.

Never neglect preparation

Bernard Shaw may have said that '*the only golden rule is that there are no golden rule*s', but here – to use an old device – there are three: preparation, preparation and preparation.

It really does make all the difference.

To begin with, preparation may seem like a chore. Certainly it can be time consuming. But if you evolve a systematic and consistent approach to how you prepare (the comment on preparation was at pains to make the point that, providing it accommodates certain essentials, it is what suits you best that matters most here) – then it will not only be useful, it will get easier and quicker to do. Good preparation is both a sound foundation to your presentations, and knowing that it has been thoroughly done is a boost to your confidence.

Practice

This book has not disguised the fact that presentation is a practical business, success cannot come simply from reading a book – though my intention was certainly that this one should help – it also demands practice. Sometimes this is in the form of rehearsal – from trying it out on the bathroom mirror to having a dry run with colleagues. It also means learning from experience.

For some people a good idea here is to *contrive* practice. Let me explain that. I know people who make very few presentations. Their job simply does not demand more. Yet when they do them, they are very important. So in some organisations steps are taken to get round the low rate of experience that results from this. For example, I have suggested to more than one of my clients that they use internal meetings to help develop skills. And I can think of one where it became mandatory for a while for formal inputs to such meetings to be made only if the participant stood up (and in another case if at least one slide was used). The good results were noticeable, such actions accelerated the practice and skills improved more quickly than they would have in the normal course of events.

A similar case might be made for certain more formal occasions or invitations. Are you, for instance, currently turning down requests to speak at any sort of event on the grounds that it is not sufficiently important for you to take on? And would it be more accurate to say you just do not want, or do not have the confidence, to do it? What could – should – you take on, in part for the experience it will give you? No presentation, no practice is hardly a recipe for improving standards.

Practice may include some further study, and this is a well provided for area of business literature. But there is another element of practice that should be mentioned before we end: training.

The best training in this topic involves skill development, and thus practice, and is best done using video recording equipment to allow individual participants to see what they do and learn from a critique of it; a critique by themselves as much as by others. I conduct courses on the subject regularly, both as public seminars and as in-company workshops (and there are, of course a profusion of sources of such training). A course can provide a short, sharp 'kick-start' that for some people is invaluable. Sometimes it can replace months of floundering around uncertain quite how to improve what is done. The pay off can be rapid and worthwhile (as, for example, with a customer presentation of some sort that successfully wins business). Training can be useful whether you are making a start on the process or have experience, but simply want to check and extend that experience. I, again in common I am sure with other consultants, also regularly get asked to help with the preparation and rehearsal of particular presentations, where short tutorial sessions either for team presentation or for individuals can be helpful and cost effective.

Working on a presentation is certainly an activity where you can get so close to things that you cease to see the wood for the trees. An objective view (which might equally be from a colleague within the organisation as from a consultant) can help move things along in a way that repeated private rehearsal may not.

And finally

At the end of the day, after all is said and done, when push comes to shove... sorry no false endings. A final few words. If you understand the principles involved, the tricks of the trade as it were. If you are well prepared in every sense – whether it is in terms of having thought through what to say, how to say it and what materials to have in front of you while you do so, or are just comfortable with the environment and not worrying about how to stand or whether your slides will be legible from the back of the room – then your presentation will stand a good chance of going well.

And that is all there is to it. Well, at least it is more than enough to get you started, indeed to get you well under way. Even the most practised and accomplished presenter can continue to learn as long as they continue to present. So perhaps the last thing to be said is that you should actively plan to go on learning from experience. Good habits help. After every presentation there will be some-thing to note. If you make a point of noting it – *I must find a better way of explaining that – that's clearly a good description, I mustn't forget it* – then you will always be able to say that you were satisfied with your last presentation (even if never one hundred per cent satisfied!). And know that your next one will be even better.

So, what next? Ready? – Take a couple of deep breaths, maybe a sip of water, look your audience in their collective eyes and begin – *Good morning...*